Emotional Intelligence Primal Leadership 2.0

Discover Why EQ Applied Matter More Than IQ Boosting Your Social, Conversation, and People Skills for Relationships, Project Managers, and Sales

Robin T. Schneider

Contents

Introduction

Everyone has some intuitive notion of a definition of Intelligence but we usually express our understanding by reciting a list of related ideas and words. Words like Genius and Creativity come to mind but there are a lot more. We feel comfortable as laypeople in discussing Intelligence because we are not burdened with too much knowledge on the subject. We do not demand an exact definition.

People like psychologists, neuroscientists and other experts may not have our comfort level because they understand all about what it is and what it is not. However, even the experts have difficulty giving a short succinct definition for it. Maybe they know so much even they can't define it either.

Are geniuses intelligent? Yeah, probably most of the time but not on all topics. The list of people referred to as geniuses certainly includes people like Leonardo da Vinci, Wolfgang Amadeus Mozart and Albert Einstein. However, that does not mean they were geniuses at everything. They often have difficult personalities, may lack social skills and some even had very unhappy lives. For example, Mozart, regarded as a musical genius, was deeply in debt at his death because he was not intelligent about his finances. It has been reported that Albert Einstein had such a short memory he sometimes could not be trusted to find his way home. Some also have areas of weakness in topics other than that of their genius. So, how do genius and intelligence relate to each other? That depends on how you define intelligence.

Wow! Now that is another long list of words that Wikipedia recites. Still not what you might call a succinct definition. It is more of a description than a definition so we should not be upset that we can't define it either. However, you should get the general idea. Intelligence is the ability to function in our environment and our world. Some people seem to have a lot of it and others, not so much. Notice that the definition of intelligence does not speak of education. After all, people without an advanced education function fully in our environment and meet the descriptors above from Wikipedia. Having a higher education does not guarantee intelligence; in fact, we have all heard of 'educated fools,' people with lots of higher education but are unable to apply common sense.

We can be certain that the human brain is the seat of intelligence but it is extremely complicated. Neuroscientists specialize in understanding the brain. However, intelligence is a combination of the 'wet ware,' that is the actual organ along with many other components that include experiences and the ability to interpret and use the knowledge contained therein.

To understand intelligence, we need to understand how the human brain works, beginning with the physiology. The following chapters describe the human brain in simple terms that should be easy for anyone, with an advanced education or not, to understand. For most of us, this means learning some new terms and concepts, but it is not necessary for us to study neuroscience.

Chapter 1:
What is Emotional Intelligence

Nowadays, people are more aware of their emotions. We have entered an age where in a profound understanding of how we feel and how others feel is essential at home, in school, in the workplace and with the many relationships we form during the course of our lifetime. Psychologists and sociological experts agree that logical intelligence alone is not the only gauge of an individual's maturity and reliability. Employers understand that applicants with a high emotional intelligence level are more likely to succeed in their chosen careers than those who have outstanding recommendations but fail to get along with others.

This section highlights what emotional intelligence is, how much we know about it and why it is important. This chapter will prepare you for the rest of the book's contents and will introduce you to concepts as well as terms often used in the discussion of emotional intelligence.

What is Emotional Intelligence?

Emotional intelligence is the ability used by individuals to gauge, understand and control their emotions, as well as those of their peers (What Is Emotional Intelligence, Daniel Goleman, 2018). Some theorists and psychologists hold strongly to the belief that emotional intelligence – or EI – is an inborn trait, while others say that it can be trained, improved and even degraded.

Why is Emotional Intelligence Important?

Our entire lives revolve around happiness, satisfaction, despair, loss and achievement. These are just a few of the emotions that dictate how we react to certain situations. Our identity and the people we meet do not matter, we will always be in touch with how we feel, just as much as we are aware of how we think. It is easy to see the use and importance of emotional intelligence.

Individuals who have a high level of emotional intelligence can easily relate their feelings to others, inasmuch as they can understand what others are feeling. This facilitates better communication between individuals and groups and strengthens relationships — whether familial, professional or romantic. Furthermore, people who are aware of the importance of emotional intelligence have been proven to have better control of their emotions. They are less prone to engage in arguments or petty fights and are more diplomatic when it comes to handling sensitive issues such as religion or race.

A person's emotional intelligence speaks volumes about their personality and maturity. People with relatively low emotional intelligence are not only more impatient, irate and immature; they are also more prone to be depressed or anxious. On the other hand, people with high or at least average levels of emotional intelligence have the ability to arrive at well-thought decisions based on facts, and not on emotional bias. Several studies have proven that emotional intelligence is directly linked to a person's ability to be successful in his or her career, and to form lasting, meaningful relationships with others.

Overall, emotional intelligence and a high awareness of it are important because they contribute greatly to the personal development of an individual. In effect, an individual's emotions and control also affect the people in his or her social circles. You will get an overview of the benefits in the sections to follow.

History

A ballpark base for emotional intelligence came into being in 1983 when Harvard psychologist Howard Gardner presented his 'Theory of Multiple Intelligences' which laid the foundation for different types of intelligence models. It described interpersonal intelligence and intrapersonal intelligence. Interpersonal intelligence is an individual's ability to understand the motivations, needs and intentions of others. Intrapersonal intelligence, on the other hand, was defined as a person's capacity to gain an understanding of his or her own fears, emotions and motivations. This set the stage for a more widespread and universally popular psychological concept related to a person's ability to manage emotions.

The term 'emotional intelligence' was initially created by university professors and researchers Pater Salovey and John D. Mayer in 1990 (Virkus, 2009). They described it as a type of social intelligence that comprises the ability to identify your own and others' emotions to distinguish between them and leverage this information for guiding one's own thoughts and actions.

Though the researcher duo developed a couple of tests to measure an individual's emotional intelligence, they aren't widely known outside the academic community. The person more famously associated with emotional intelligence as a term and concept is Daniel Goleman, as previously mentioned.

In 1990, behavior science writer Daniel Goleman reinforced Salovey and Mayer's work in his path-breaking book, Emotional Intelligence. Goleman was a behavior science journalist specializing in mind, emotions and behavior research for Popular Psychology and later the New York Times. He studied psychology at Harvard University, working closely with David McClelland and other eminent behavior experts. McClelland was from a group of prominent university researchers who were looking out for intelligence test alternatives, owing to the view that these tests revealed little about the traits that are required to gain overall success in life.

While researching for his book on emotions and evolved emotional literacy, Goleman chanced upon the findings of Salovey and Mayer. According to an Annie Paul article, Goleman obtained permission from the behavior experts for using the 'emotional intelligence' term in his book. The permission was swiftly granted subject to the condition that Goleman would make it clear where he originally came across the term. While earlier the book was to be a discussion on 'emotional literacy,' Salovey-Mayer's research inspired Goleman to focus on emotional intelligence.

Goleman debated that it wasn't cognitive intelligence alone, which guaranteed an individual's success in life. He emphasized the importance of emotional intelligence that awarded people four characteristics – 1. Understanding your own emotions, 2. Managing your own emotions, 3. Being empathetic to other's emotions, 4. Handling others' emotions by demonstrating high social skills.

Daniel Goleman's book promoted the idea of emotional intelligence as more powerful than intelligence quotient in predicting an individual's life success. Emotional intelligence as a concept became so revolutionary and significant that the book sold a whopping 5 million copies within the initial five years itself. The world lapped up the concept of emotional intelligence with both hands. Though the book emphasized on the importance of emotional intelligence in everyday life, work and relationship success, it didn't throw much light on how to identify one's and others' emotions. There wasn't a cohesive theory on describing core human emotions. Also, the book didn't offer information about increasing one's emotional intelligence.

In 1998 Daniel Goleman published another book titled 'Working with Emotional Intelligence,' which sought to widen the emotional intelligence definition. He broadened the scope of the concept of emotional intelligence to include 25 skills, core competencies and abilities.

One of the biggest criticisms that came in the way of Goleman's theory was that emotions can be highly complex, multi-layered and often limited by any language's inability to describe them. Even languages featuring the most extensive vocabulary sometimes fall short when it comes to assigning labels to specific emotions for self-reflection or interpersonal communication. The Salovey-Mayer tests encompass a few broad emotions and feelings that are limited by the inability to articulate the exactness of some of the most complex/multi-dimensional feelings/emotions.

Though the concept of emotional quotient is widely received and extremely relevant today, the measuring of emotional intelligence scores through tests has always been under the scanner. The Salovey-Mayer emotional intelligence test team themselves stated that though they attempt to measure an individual's emotional intelligence through a series of evaluations on paper, it is hard to tell if the individual would act in a similar manner in real-life scenarios or when subjected to extreme conditions/stress. These may be the very situations in which he or she may need high emotional intelligence. So, tests measuring a person's emotional intelligence may gauge actions in regular situations and not situations of extreme duress when he or she actually needs to display developed emotional intelligence.

Goleman, Salovey and other pioneers in the behavior sciences field met to discuss the latest research and best practices at the 5th Annual Nexus EQ Conference in the Netherlands in 2005, called 'Leading with Emotional Intelligence: Tools and Wisdom for a Sustainable World.' It featured experts from 19 nations and was the most inclusive Emotional Quotient global summit. The 2013 Nexus EQ Conference hosted at Harvard University featured participation from 32 nations.

Several corporate bottom line studies have demonstrated that the ability to get the best out of people directly affects the company's profit performance. Research revealed that L'Oréal sales representatives selected on the basis of higher emotional competencies recorded an increase in annual net sales revenue by $2, 558,360.

A Brief on Emotions

With the study of emotional intelligence inevitably comes discussion and debate which focus on emotions. What are emotions? Where do they come from? How do they work? This section will explore, in brief, the basic questions people often ask about the complexity of human emotions.

What are Emotions?

Psychologically speaking, an emotion is a state that involves thoughts, actions and experiences. This broad definition of what an emotion is has, to this day, not yet been entirely resolved because of the problematic nature of emotions themselves. Usually, people relate a specific emotion as one of the results of a certain event or trigger. For example, if an individual fails an important exam, he or she may experience the emotions of anger, disappointment, depression, sadness or frustration. In fact, the individual may experience those emotions and more altogether.

Several psychologists have tried to capture the essence of emotions in a single sentence or phrase; however, there is still no one definition for emotions except that they are states where the mind enters upon an encounter or experience. The paragraphs below will briefly discuss some of the theories that aim to explain how emotions work.

The James-Lange Theory

The James-Lange theory of emotion, proposed by the 19th century scholars William James and Carl Lange, states that experiences are the basis of all human emotions (Cherry, 2018). Through their theory, James and Lange illustrated how experiences cause physiological changes such as heart rate and muscular tension. In turn, these physical reactions trigger the brain to interpret the experience or situation in a certain way. The brain's consequent interpretations of those experiences give birth to different emotions.

The Cannon-Bard Theory

Contrary to the beliefs of James and Lange, Walter Cannon and Philip Bard suggested that the physical reactions of the body to certain experiences happen immediately after, or in the same period as, the brain's interpretation of the event (Cherry, Understanding the Cannon-Bard Theory of Emotion, 2018).

The Lazarus Theory

This theory simply states that, to trigger an emotion, a recurring thought must first be interpreted and released by the brain to the other parts of the body. For example, imagine that you are a six-year-old child who has just heard horror stories from your cousins. Your parents have requested you to go to bed. The lights in your room are all off; there is no night lamp to comfort you. You hear strange sounds coming from outside your bedroom window. You start to think that a ghost or a monster, such as the ones from your cousins' stories, is out there waiting to get you.

The thought that there are ghosts or monsters just outside your bedroom window triggers physical reactions from your body. You begin to sweat and tremble. At the same time, you feel fear and apprehension. The Lazarus theory suggests that individuals cannot have emotions if there are no thoughts to act as triggers and experiences to be thought about.

The Facial-Feedback Theory

The Facial-Feedback theory states that emotions are the results of the changes in our facial muscles. Simply speaking, smiling or grinning makes us feel happy, while frowning makes us feel angry. The changes in our facial muscles serve as cues for the brain to interpret and name the emotions that we experience.

Benefits of EQ

Now that we understand what exactly emotional intelligence is and its brief history, let's discuss the benefits of this super psychological tonic in everyday life. How does having a high emotional quotient or emotional intelligence impact our everyday life? What are the benefits of possessing well-developed emotional intelligence? How can it be leveraged to make our lives more meaningful and rewarding? How can it bring us greater success at work and in business, as well as more harmonious interpersonal relationships? Some advantages of being an emotional intelligent individual include:

Positively Handling Change

Emotionally intelligent people are brilliant at responding to change. Their awareness of the situation, controlled reactions and understanding the merits/demerits of the change help them remain unperturbed and handle the change more effectively. They are aware of the fact that though one can't control one's circumstances, one can control his/her reaction to it. Emotionally intelligent people will often make the most of these changes to benefit them. Their response to changing people, circumstances and events remains positive.

Conflict Resolution

The reason emotional intelligence is such a sought-after factor in the corporate world is that it equips managers with the ability to deal with a challenging workforce and situations. Leaders must possess social skills in the form of empathy, motivation, self-awareness and awareness of other's emotions to resolve conflicts successfully. Leaders must be able to inspire loyalty and this comes by empathizing with people and understanding their inherent needs. You can resolve conflicts efficiently by displaying superior negotiation skills, empathy, positivity, assertiveness and understanding. You can emphasize on the overall good if you are empathetic yet assertive. As a leader, you also need to understand how your emotions and behavior affect the situation and direct your actions to better manage the crisis. You have to work with others to take more positive decisions for the over-all good.

Boosts Self-Motivation

Self-awareness and self-regulation are the cornerstone of emotional intelligence. When we are able to understand and manage our emotions more effectively, we know how to keep ourselves motivated. Emotionally intelligent people know what drives them and hence find it easier to achieve goals they set their sights on. There is a greater commitment, initiative and readiness to take action. Such people also display greater resilience, determination and optimism when it comes to achieving their goals. They are more organized, display better time management skills, have a higher sense of priority and are more assertive when things come in the way of their goals.

More Collaboration Less Competition

Emotionally intelligent people are generally high on self-confidence and self-esteem. They know their strengths and weakness, and are able to manage them successfully. They don't suffer from insecurities or a false sense of self-importance. They don't feel the need to reinforce their abilities and superiority by competing with others or showing them down. An emotionally evolved individual incites more collaboration than competition. His or her focus is on the overall positive outcome of a situation and not individual victories. Sportspersons possessing a high emotional quotient will keep aside their personal scores and records, and play for the overall benefit of their team. Their actions will be in tandem with what's good for the team and not their individual performance or accolades. Emotional intelligence equips you with the power to collaborate more and compete less with people. It rids you of the one-upmanship syndrome to drive you to do what's beneficial for everyone involved.

Boosts Sales for an Organization

A bunch of emotionally intelligent salespersons will be able to display greater understanding of the needs, emotions, fears, challenges, driving factors and aspirations of their target audience. This will help them create more impactful and compelling sales pitches which will appeal to their potential customers. When you know the core emotions of your market, you will know how to adjust your campaigns to get people to listen to your marketing message. A study of more than 40 Fortune 500 firms concluded that sales personnel with high emotional quotient/emotional intelligence out-did those with average to low emotional intelligence by about 50%. Emotional intelligence helps you empathize with your audience before selling to them, and thus increase the organization's overall sales.

Enhances Overall Well-Being

Imagine a scenario where your manager has admonished you early in the morning for a task that wasn't performed up to the mark even when you know you've put in your best. How would you feel? How would you react? What would you think? People low on emotional intelligence will start having doubts about their abilities, will be more prone to stress over the incident throughout the day and generally display a foul mood by letting the situation get the better of them. However, people with high emotional intelligence will not take it personally. They will be more aware of their manager's stress, penchant for perfection and go-getter attitude. They will know it's not so much about their capability as the need of the other person to be the best.

Emotionally intelligent people understand others' needs and emotions enough to not blame themselves for everything and stress over the smallest of things. In this case, rather than fuming, they will try and understand what exactly the manager wants and more importantly why he/she wants it. They will then manage their emotions and reactions in response to others' emotions to arrive at the most positive outcome. This helps you manage your reactions, decreases stress, boosts positivity and improves your overall well-being.

More Conditioned for Success

People with a high emotional quotient are more conditioned to be successful in life. They are intrinsically motivated, less prone to procrastination, display higher self-confidence, are better negotiators and conflict resolvers, and are more focused on their goals. They know how to deal with their and others' emotions to build more supportive networks. Emotionally intelligent people are able to overcome setbacks more efficiently and are more perseverant while handling challenging situations. They possess a more resilient outlook and know how to control their reactions in circumstances they can't control.

A company operating in a particular region decides to terminate the services of people belonging to a certain community for vested interests. Now, if you are a person belonging to the community, you are aware it's beyond your circle of control that you were born into the community. You can't change your origins and can do little about the situation (other than fighting a legal battle). However, even when emotionally intelligent people cannot influence their circumstances, they are savvy enough to choose their reaction to these circumstances. They quickly grab the next best opportunity by channeling their actions more positively rather than mulling over things where they have little control. They rule over circumstances rather than letting circumstances get the better of them, due to which they are more slated for success.

Enhances Leadership Skills

Emotionally intelligent people have a well-developed knack for understanding others and identifying factors that motivate them. They then use this information positively to forge greater loyalty and stronger bonds. An able leader can understand the needs, emotions and aspirations of her or his people. They know how to direct this understanding to encourage better performances and people satisfaction. An emotionally savvy manager will be able to create stronger, more motivated and loyal teams by strategically using the team's emotional diversity. They will intuitively harness the strengths and weaknesses of the team for optimal overall benefit.

Individuals who are emotionally intelligent have the ability to manage their emotions better and this makes them less prone to outbursts, and more focused on assertiveness, which automatically earns them greater respect. When we master self and other people's emotions, we know exactly how to direct them to create more harmonious surroundings.

Better Relationships

Emotional intelligence helps us enjoy better relationships by being aware of our and others' feelings, thoughts, emotions and behavior. We can communicate in a more positive and constructive manner to forge stronger interpersonal bonds. Gaining an awareness of the needs, responses and emotions of our loved ones leads to more fulfilling and gratifying relationships. Emotional intelligence helps us show empathy, makes us less aggressive and helps us manage conflicts within the relationship more efficiently. We find ourselves resorting to less manipulation, aggression, submission and power games. Emotional intelligence makes us confident enough to assert our rights within a relationship without damaging the other person. It awards us the ability to balance conflicting situations to maintain a positive and harmonious environment. The ability to manage our emotions in relation to others makes us react/respond to people we care for in a more thoughtful and empathetic manner. When we are able to relate to others in a more efficient manner, we form better and more lasting relationships.

Let's consider a scenario. 'A' and 'B' are involved in a serious romantic relationship. 'A' is more gregarious, social, and has lots of friends due to an amicable and easy-going nature. 'B' is more of a thoughtful introvert who enjoys reading, meditation, and bonds with a group of selected friends. 'B' doesn't take too well to 'A's' time out with friends, social media activity and generally being accessible to everyone.

Now, if 'A' isn't emotionally intelligent, 'A' will simply label 'B' as insecure, jealous and possessive, inviting more conflict within the relationship. Let's now assume 'A' has a high emotional intelligence. 'A' will be likelier to understand where 'B' is coming from, what 'B's' insecurities are and why 'B' thinks the way 'B' does. 'A' will make a greater attempt to involve 'B' in social activities to make 'B' feel a part of it. 'A' will take time out to discuss feelings and arrive at a more positive plan of action that benefits both. There will be an attempt to put forth 'A's' view of wanting some time out with friends without hurting 'B's' feelings. Rather than blaming others, emotionally intelligent people attempt to understand them and arrive at a middle ground, which is beneficial for everyone involved.

In the above scenario, 'A' may keep aside some days exclusively for 'B,' while working out a way to go out with friends once a week so 'B' doesn't feel neglected. This way, 'A' has used knowledge of 'B's' emotions and feelings to empathize and to arrive at a solution that makes them both feel better, which allows them to share a more meaningful and fulfilling relationship.

Boosts Physical Health
This one's a no-brainer. When we are mentally happy, it reflects on our bodies. Emotionally intelligent folks are able to control their emotions and cope with stress more constructively. They don't try and control what's outside their circle of control, but are able to manage their reaction to the stressful stimuli. This leads to better emotional health, and subsequently glowing physical health, since an individual's mental health is closely tied with their physical well-being.

Enhanced Communication Skills

Individuals with a high emotional quotient are able to articulate themselves better according to the needs and aspirations of other people. They have the ability to listen to people, which is one of the most significant aspects of communication. They understand what to say to manage pulling the heartstrings of people. Emotionally intelligent folks know what motivates people and structure their message accordingly to elicit the most positive response. They are masters at inspiring people to take actions. Teams are likelier to listen and respond to a more emotionally savvy leader, who understands their feelings rather than a technically competent leader who fails to empathize with them or make an emotional connect.

Less Prone to Addiction

Addictions are typically a result of our failure to deal with our emotions. The inability to deal with underlying emotions and feelings makes life tougher for a person, which often results in turning to substances to 'help them cope.' It is often under-developed emotional intelligence that leads people to addiction, and gets them stuck in a miserable pattern. Even sobriety on the face of it is only a temporary solution, unless the addict develops emotional intelligence. People who aim to get rid of their addictions can be more successful if they tackle the underlying emotions that lead to it by gaining more self-awareness.

Such individuals who are emotionally intelligent are aware of their strengths and weaknesses. They have a good understanding of their feelings and emotional make-up. They are aware of the emotions be-hind their actions. They don't struggle with their feelings and their inability to cope with it. Emotional intelligence equips you with the ca-pacity to deal with your emotions in a more positive manner by gain-ing complete awareness of it. People who possess high emotional in-telligence are mostly confident, happy and fulfilled. They don't feel the need to depend on anything other than themselves for their chal-lenges and inabilities. Emotionally intelligent people are less prone to use substances as coping mechanisms because they are emotionally self-sufficient and more adaptable to change. They know how to cope with complicated situations based on their understanding of their and others' emotions. They've mastered the art of managing their emo-tions to adapt to and cope with changes around them to bring more positivity in their lives. When a person is mentally strong, emotionally self-sufficient and has complete awareness of their feelings, s/he is less likely to seek the recourse of external factors such as abusive relationships, drugs, alcohol and other similar addictions.

Difference Between EQ and IQ

Imagine yourself as a manager leading a team of a few competent, talented and highly qualified individuals. Your team has been assigned a rather challenging client contract that if done well, can be a huge achievement for the firm. Trouble is, it involves a lot of hard work, hours of research, staying up after work hours and working on week-ends. As a leader, you're proficient enough to deliver all the technical training and expertise required to complete the task. But how can you persuade your great team to work on the project more positively and without getting them petulant about the entire project?

Your technical expertise, ability and knowledge will help you impart technical skills but it won't help you successfully motivate them to fulfill the task at hand. You may solve all their technical problems, come up with expert industry solutions and even expand their skill base. How will you get them to complete the project in a rewarding, inspired, productive and positive manner? Enter – emotional intelligence.

While your technical expertise is a result of your intelligence, quotient and ability, your ability to manage your team's behavior for the organization's benefit by gaining complete awareness of their emotions is emotional intelligence. By engaging in a deeper and better understanding of their feelings, thoughts and behavior, you can better manage their behavior to your advantage. When you know what motivates people, how they react to certain situations, why they behave the way they do, the underlying emotions behind their actions and other similar insights, you will be able to direct your behavior more productively. This is the main difference between IQ and EQ.

Though a person's IQ determines his/her competencies and unique capabilities, his/her EQ determines how s/he will interact with and treat other people. It demonstrates how an individual will deal with pressures or crisis.

Intelligence is a measure of your cognitive abilities such as logical thinking, problem solving, analytical thinking, memorizing and creativity. Emotional intelligence, on the other hand, is being aware of and managing your and others' emotions for optimal positive results. While IQ measures the mathematical, verbal and logical prowess of a person, EQ reinforces their ability to form balanced interpersonal relationships in both their personal and professional life. It encompasses empathy, stress management, integrity, intuition and flexibility. Emotional quotient tests emphasize questions related to one's emotions in different situations and other people, while IQ questions focus on our reasoning skills and logical abilities. It is often said that while IQ ensures success throughout your academic life, EQ ensures overall life success.

Let's take another example to illustrate the difference between the two concepts. You know there's a huge problem of uninspired workforce in your workplace, due to which performance is suffering. Your employees are simply not motivated enough to work. You are aware of all the facts, statistics and reasons for the poor performance. That's your intelligence quotient. When you are able to use these facts for motivating your employees to boost their performance, you display a more evolved emotional quotient. Simply being aware of facts but not displaying empathy with the employees is a demonstration of high IQ but low EQ. However, when you use the knowledge and facts for appealing to your employees' emotions, you're showing high EQ.

An individual's EQ determines how he or she interacts with people. Therefore, it has a huge bearing on their happiness and success. People who possess a higher EQ tend to know how to direct people's actions by appealing to their emotions and reasons. A major difference is that though one can't change their intelligence, they can learn to manage his/her and others' emotions to lead a more successful and rewarding life.

A fundamental difference between IQ and EQ is that while IQ is inborn (influenced largely by genetics), EQ can be developed. An individual's reasoning powers and logical abilities cannot be altered by a large degree. However, the ability to handle emotions and manage them to your advantage can be learned. This is the biggest advantage of EQ over IQ. EQ gives you greater flexibility to change situations, people and your life by optimally managing your and others' emotions. While IQ is arguably something that's primarily outside your circle of control, EQ can be cultivated to increase your career and personal relationship prospects.

People with higher EQ can successfully express, control and identify their emotions, assess other people's emotions and have a greater capacity to perceive emotions in general. People with a high intelligence quotient show a marked ability to absorb, comprehend and apply knowledge. They also possess higher logical reasoning, creativity and abstract thinking faculties.

Though we've seen how research has pointed to EQ as the single largest factor for success at work, both IQ and EQ are important in their respective ways. Sometimes, gaining an awareness of your and others' behavior for managing emotions can be futile if not backed by technical expertise. IQ is closely connected with the mind's nourishment and manifested during our academic years. EQ is more developed over a period of time based on our experiences and learned behavior. However, what makes EQ more sought after for the corporate world today is that while almost everyone qualified and trained for a job possess the same required expertise, it is EQ that helps companies distinguish the average workforce from future leaders. It is something that can be constantly developed, is more complex and encompasses a wider range of behavior pattern controllers.

People with a high EQ are generally self-confident, possess greater self-awareness, and are able to handle challenging emotional experiences more efficiently. This is why EQ has a correlation with a person's chances of workplace success and interpersonal relationships. Individuals with a more evolved EQ are better able to identify and manage their own emotions, while also recognizing other's emotional states to adjust to them accordingly.

Unlike IQ, the worth of emotional intelligence is not immediately apparent. IQ is more conspicuous in our academics, performance tests, memory skills, intelligence testing games and other cognitive activities. However, your ability to better manage emotions is not obvious or even easily measurable. How can you gauge if a person is emotionally intelligent other than subjecting them to psychological tests? The results of an emotionally intelligent decision are not as apparent as intelligent quotient driven decisions because emotions are difficult to name and measure. Since they are so complex and multi-layered, the sheer challenge of identifying them had regaled them to secondary position compared to a more easily measurable intelligence factor in the early years of psychological studies. IQ was believed to be more clear-cut and therefore easier to measure and gauge. EQ can never be precisely measured even with the most path-breaking tests. You may gain rough insights on the emotional make-up of an individual, but seldom an exact mind map of the emotional patterns of a person.

Politicians and advertisers harness the power of emotional intelligence brilliantly to influence masses to make purchases or vote in their favor. Ad agencies quite successfully manipulate emotions such as fear and aspirations to accomplish their client's objectives by using information about their target audience's emotions and how these emotions function for influencing voting or buyer behavior.

Emotional intelligence is distinct from one's intellect in the sense that it taps into the fundamental elements of human behavioral patterns.

Also, there is no established connection between intelligence quotient and emotional quotient. You just can't predict an individual's EQ based on their smartness. Also, your IQ will be the same at age 15 as it will be at age 60. Emotional intelligence, on the other hand, will most likely evolve over the years according to practice and experiences. It is a more flexible set.

Some psychologists are of the opinion that regular measures of intelligence are too constricted to include a complete range of intelligence parameters. Instead, they suggest that the power to comprehend and express emotions plays an equally important if not greater role in determining the chances of an individual's success.

Your intelligence quotient is calculated with the help of standardized intelligence tests. It is measured by dividing a person's mental age by his or her chronological age and subsequently multiplying the number by 100. For instance, a 10-year-old child possessing a mental age of 16 will have an IQ of 160. Scores of many IQ tests today are measured by comparatively analyzing an individual's score with the scores of others within the same chronological age group.

Though there are many studies to calculate emotional intelligence, the Mayer Salovey Caruso Emotional Intelligence Test (MSCEIT) is known to be the most comprehensive measure of an individual's EQ. It was the result of an intelligence-testing legacy established due to a scientific awareness of human emotions with the intention of gauging an individual's emotional intelligence. The four scales that are used to evaluate emotional intelligence in the MSCEIT test include perceiving emotions, understanding emotions, facilitating thoughts and managing emotions.

Research undertaken by the Carnegie Institute of Technology demonstrated that 85% of one's financial success is due to human engineering skills, communication abilities, negotiating abilities, leadership skills and personality. Surprisingly, a mere 15% was attributed to technical knowledge. Nobel Prize winning psychologist Daniel Kahneman discovered people are more willing to do business with people they like and can trust even if they offer lower quality products/services or products/services for a higher price.

Though IQ is recognized as a vital attribute for success, specifically for academic achievements, experts have recognized that it's not the sole determinant for a successful life. It is a single component in a huge field of complex influences including emotional intelligence and other factors.

While hiring, companies look for a person's EQ over IQ. A high IQ helps you build interpersonal skills only until a certain degree. It gives you the knowledge, technical finesse and industry expertise to perform your job optimally. EQ is more geared towards your character and emotions based in the manner through which you respond to your colleagues, reply to your e-mails, collaborate with your team, network with contemporaries, lead and instruct subordinates, and work towards fulfilling the organization's goals.

Chapter 2:
Emotional Intelligence Basics

Human characteristics that are innate are those which one is born with and from which instinctual responses are derived. A debate exists as to whether emotional intelligence is inborn and is part of a person's personality, or whether it can be acquired in adulthood even when one did not previously have it.

The term personality is used in psychology to refer to an individual's thoughts, emotions, behaviors and attitudes that are unique to that person. Emotions, especially, are a core aspect of the subject of this book. For example, some people are by nature happy, talkative and full of energy, while others can be described as having a steady, calm and reliable disposition. This is to mean that personality influences introversion and extroversion tendencies in people.

The reason why the subject of personality is of importance here is due to the fact that it is inborn or innate. Although we can improve on our personalities, the changes incurred will be very slight and will tend not to vary much from whom we innately are. Emotional intelligence on the other hand may involve the application of already present natural abilities into practical everyday situations, such as in exercising sound judgment based on clear thinking patterns.

Whereas two people may share common tendencies in reference to their personalities, the manner in which they apply themselves to real-life situations will tend to be very different. For example, of two individuals with a melancholic personality, one may possess very high levels of personal motivation and ambition while the other one may not.

If as a manager you are seeking to employ someone as a salesperson, conducting a personality test will not be sufficient although it may show that the person is talkative and friendly enough to make contacts and sales. There would be a need to know how a person would cope under the pressure that comes with deadlines, and that they will persist in the face of insurmountable challenges and work-related disappointments. A test of their emotional intelligence would equip you with that kind of information.

An employee may have a very pleasant and 'fun' personality but that does not necessarily equate to being a success at the workplace. Employees who possess high emotional intelligence levels will be able to manage and control negative impulses that stem from their personalities in such a way as to bring themselves work-related success.

Some studies claim that human beings are to a certain degree born with a measure of emotional intelligence, which they term as 'innate emotional intelligence.' They point to an infant's ability for emotional sensitivity, as well the potential they have to retain and later recall all the emotional information that they are taking in from their environments during infancy. This information later forms the core of an individual's emotional intelligence.

An infant emotionally learns over time to sense when its mother is angry because they associate some of her repetitive reactions to anger. As they grow, this stored information forms the basis from which they are able to sense other people's feelings. This so-called 'innate intelligence' can be continually developed or damaged through life experiences.

It is very possible for an infant to start life with some degree of emotional intelligence and then unlearn it by imitating unhealthy emotional tendencies from his caregivers. Unhealthy environments of abuse and neglect can also contribute to this unlearning process. Similarly, some infants may show low levels of emotional sensitivity but with the right emotional nurturing, end up scoring very high as emotionally intelligent adults.

EI/EQ Framework

Now that you know the definition, importance and history of emotional intelligence, you are ready to learn about its characteristics as stated by the American psychologist Daniel Goleman. Knowing the characteristics of EI will help you reach a better, deeper understanding of how you can manage your own emotions. This section will also give you a good idea of the current level of your EI.

The Five Elements of Emotional Intelligence

According to Daniel Goleman, people with average or high emotional intelligence levels share the following characteristics (Emotional Intelligence Theory: Highlighting and Developing Leadership Skills, 2016). Below is the framework designed by Goleman to show the five basic elements of EI:

Self-Awareness

Self-awareness, as defined in psychology, is the state in which individuals become cognizant of their physical, mental and spiritual or emotional traits. It is among the first components geared towards building an individual's self-concept. The other two components of an individual's self-concept are self-esteem and the ideal self.

Researchers have long tried to pinpoint when an individual first gains self-awareness. The psychologists Lewis and Brooks-Gun performed what is now known as the 'Rouge Test' on infants of varying ages. The test involved dabbing the infant's nose with a red dot, and then placing the infant in front of a mirror to check whether he or she would reach for his or her own nose. The individuals who reached for their noses during this test were evidence that they already had a measure of self-awareness.

Lewis and Brooks-Gun observed that there were almost no children under the age of one year who would consciously reach for their noses while looking at their reflection. Only 25% of toddlers aged 15 to 18 months reached for their noses during the test, while 75% of toddlers between the ages of 21 to 24 months touched their noses in recognition.

A person displaying a high level of emotional intelligence usually also has a high degree of self-awareness. Such individuals are capable of understanding their emotions, of putting situations into perspective, and of seeing themselves as others might view them. Because they understand their emotions better, they are less prone to bouts of low self-esteem.

Instead, individuals with a good level of self-awareness are often confident and comfortable about how they talk, look and move. This allows them to be more honest with themselves; thus, they know their respective strengths and weaknesses. Additionally, they are aware that, if they have strong points and weak points, then the people around them must also have their own set of achievements and failures.

Self-Regulation

Self-regulation refers to the consistent ability of an individual to control or manage his or her emotions. This is especially important in situations of anger, misunderstanding or rage. Self-regulation is also connected to an individual's ability to calm him or herself during particularly emotional and stressful events.

Psychologists agree that self-regulation is important in the growth of an individual. Without a certain measure of self-regulation, people would be more prone to lashing out, arguing and engaging in dangerous activities. Self-regulation should be taught and practiced during childhood. The child must learn how to evaluate what he or she is feeling, and be knowledgeable enough to discern whether his or her emotions will lead to good or bad results. With self-regulation comes the all-important ability to say 'no.'

An emotionally intelligent person has a good grasp of self-regulation. He or she is able to think effectively before acting and speaking, is thoughtful and mindful of others' feelings and is less impulsive than others. People with a high level of self-regulation often find it easy to refuse vices, bad habits and bad company.

Motivation

When it comes to motivation, none are more focused on their goals than those who are emotionally intelligent. Science has proven that people with high levels of social skills readily trade fast results for a better long-term goal. Motivated people know exactly what their goals are, what they must do to achieve those goals and how to stay focused.

Employers often look for motivated applicants because such people follow a strong cause or dream in the course of their lives. These dreams often take the form of challenges, thus making motivated people unafraid to take risks. Motivation is an important element in Goel's EI framework because it determines what kind of person an individual is and can be. Without proper motivation, people tend to give in to laziness and counter-productivity.

Empathy

It has long been known that emotionally intelligent people are not those who think too highly of themselves due to their numerous achievements, but those who are able to effectively understand even the lowliest person. Empathy is the ability to feel and think the way others do, without necessarily pitying those in a depressed state.

Empathetic people are often described as good and open-minded listeners. They are excellent at handling their relationships. Such people are able to compromise with almost anyone because they have achieved a profound knowledge of what it is like to be in another person's shoes. Empathy, not sympathy, is one of the most important elements of emotional intelligence.

Social Skills

The need to form meaningful and lasting relationships with others is a trait that is inherent in the entire human population. We are social creatures. We crave communication and interaction with different people, whether they are of the same or different sex, age, race and religion. However, not all have the talent of slipping into an easy conversation with a stranger, making small talk with an acquaintance or having a genuine fun time at a party.

An emotionally intelligent individual has developed social skills. These skills were honed through experience, as well as practice. In the workplace, individuals with high social skills are often dubbed as the team leaders, the representatives and the all-round workroom friend. They are excellent in balancing the traits of each of their team members and act as the backbone of the team without being too bossy or demanding.

Social skills are important in the growth of any individual as these help in the formation of relationships. People who are too shy often experience trouble when it comes to making new friends, not because they do not want to, but because their social skills are not strong enough to provide them with the confidence to go out and interact with others.

Chapter 3:
Signs of Low Emotional Intelligence

Now that you are familiar with the theories, concepts and importance of emotional intelligence, you most probably want to know the level of your EI, or emotional quotient (EQ) as some call it. Below is a mini checklist designed to help you have a clearer picture regarding the degree of your emotional intelligence. Though this section is not a scientific test of your EQ, it will certainly help you to know what your weak and strong points are when it comes to emotional intelligence.

The Signs of Low EQ

People with low emotional intelligence are often described as immature and irresponsible. They sometimes act as though they own the world, or they deserve everyone's rapt, undying attention. They also exhibit traits such as impatience, indecisiveness and oversensitivity (Bradberry, n.d.).

A Person with a Low EQ:

- Is incapable of explaining his or her feelings to others, whether in written or verbal form

- Is unable to express him or herself well enough to be understood by others, thus he or she feels oppressed

- Is unable to reconcile him or herself with intense emotions such as despair, loss, agony and elation

- Lacks a sense of responsibility, integrity and sincerity

- Is rarely sensitive to the feelings of others

- Thinks emotions expressed through tears are irrational or degrading

- Is rigid when it comes to the beliefs of others

- Rarely shows sympathy or empathy

- Is unable to listen in a genuine manner to other people

- Thinks the worst of others

- Is incapable of trusting friends completely

- Lacks the strength to forgive and be forgiven

- Is afraid of responsibility

- Holds grudges with most of his or her peers

- Quickly criticizes or judges' others without first understanding the situation or individual

- Is often overly pessimistic

- Has a habit of voicing his or her doubts and regrets about him or herself, but is unwilling to listen to the woes of others

- Rarely thinks before acting or speaking

- Is rarely a team player as he or she most often acts for his or her own good only

- Makes others feel inadequate and insecure

- Presents insecurity about him or herself through repeated apologies

- They are not able to make up their mind about critical social issues

On the other hand, a person with a high EQ is a joy to be around. He or she is sensitive to his or her emotions, as they stay in tune with the feelings of others. Such a person does not shy away from responsibility, but sees it as a challenge to become greater or better.

A Person with a High EQ:

- Expresses his or her emotions clearly, whether in written or verbal form

- Is comfortable talking about what he or she feels to others

- Acknowledges that emotions play a big part in self-formation

- Is open to different ideas, beliefs and opinions

- Does not let his or her emotions cloud his or her judgment

- Is sensitive to the feelings of others

- Knows when to speak, when to keep silent, when to stay and when to leave

- Appreciates the efforts of others who try to cheer, comfort or console him or her

- Is not ashamed to cry or express frustration, anger, happiness and satisfaction

- Allows his or her feelings to lead him or her to better experiences, better choices

- Acknowledges that individuals have different ways of coping with both emotions and experiences

- Is not arrested by fear or worry

- Can identify the factors or aspects that lead him or her to stress

- Can effectively rid him or herself of negative stress

- Understands that even sadness and anger play a role in mental and emotional growth

- Is not afraid of responsibility

- Does not throw the blame on others when things go wrong

- Is comfortable when talking to strangers or acquaintances

- Knows how to draw the line between being sympathetic and empathetic

- Is motivated by his or her goals

- Is patient with the mistakes of others

- Is determined to grow into a better person

Of course, there are other signs that show whether a person has a low or high emotional quotient. The web of human emotions is so complex that there are times when individuals possessing relatively high EQs may be prone to displaying the behavior of individuals with lower EQs, and vice-versa. Remember that the first step to improving and understanding your emotional intelligence is to accept that you are not perfect in emotional stability.

Chapter 4:
Boost Self-Awareness

One of the most fundamental areas of emotional intelligence is the concept of self-awareness. It is the foundation on which the entire theory of emotional intelligence rests. To be aware of and manage others' emotions you need to be aware of your emotional patterns. Self-awareness can be gained by practicing different types of meditations and mindfulness. You can enroll for a meditation course, join a mindfulness group or hire an instructor to help you practice techniques of mindfulness. These methods can increase your awareness about your body, feelings and thoughts. You learn to tune into your innermost self to understand the rhythm of your feeling and emotions. There is a greater understanding of your emotions, and behavior patterns.

Meditation will help you on the road toward getting to know yourself better, but what else can you do to become more aware of this wonderful person you are? Well, there are several self-awareness exercises that you can use to help you and this chapter deals with those.

Keep a journal – This should be your record of all the feelings that you had over the course of a day and you can also have a section in your journal where you keep quotations that deal with things of an emotional nature. There are some amazing quotations online and printing these out or writing them into the back of your journal will help you. After you write down what you feel, if you find that any of it is negative, try to counterbalance it with positive things as well. Then, at the end of the exercise, write down what made you grateful getting up this morning. Try a list of five to start off with because these helps you to fuel yourself with positive thoughts.

Get into the habit of journaling your thoughts after practicing meditation/mindfulness exercises. Recording your feelings and thoughts increases your self-awareness and allows you to gain higher insights about your emotional framework. This will boost your emotional vocabulary, and allow you to identify and assign terms to specific emotions. You will get into the habit of consciously describing a full range of emotions at various points in time to help you develop greater awareness of your emotions. Apart from identifying emotions and describing them, this practice will also help you pay close attention to the intensity of these emotions. The better you can estimate them, the higher your chances of being able to monitor and alter these emotions efficiently.

The other thing that you need to do is create a **life program.** People get a little nervous when I say this, but it's not that complex. Try to decide where you want your life to go and if you find this is a little too difficult to start off with, at least set yourself up with some small goals each day, so that you feel a sense of achievement. This helps you to know your limitations, but it also helps you to face the world with realism and overcome emotional obstacles. If you have large jobs to do, split them down into manageable chunks, because you won't achieve many pats on the back if you always set your goals too high and can never meet them. Your life program has to include the following elements:

- A set time to get up

- Time for meditation

- Breakfast, lunch and dinner (all sat down and not eaten on the go)

- Tasks for tomorrow

- Tasks for the week

- Sufficient 'me' time

- Sufficient exercise

- Sufficient sleep time

When initiating this demanding voyage, you begin to realize that if you fuel your body with all the right things, your body responds by being less emotional and more sated in every day. Spend your 'me' time undertaking things that you like doing, or at least enjoying something for your own sake. When people forget this element of their lives, they tend to find resentment sets in and that's a very negative trait that doesn't help the emotional intelligence quota. The foods you eat fuel your body, the exercise you take fuels your energy levels and sufficient sleep helps the mind to be fully restored the next day. Even if you go through emotional events in your life, these essentials need to be a priority in order to reach that level of self-sufficiency that adds to your emotional responses to life.

Let me try to explain this in plain English. If you don't eat a balanced diet, your body responds by being less capable of performing the functions it needs to perform. If you don't sleep properly, your body cannot release the hormones that sleep allows in order to mend your body and mind. If you don't take time for yourself, you begin to feel that life is a drag and that you are not important enough when nothing can be further from the truth.

The Self-Awareness Exercise

This is something I do with all the people who come to me for help. We choose to go to a location that brings out the awe in you. It may be a beach at sunset or sunrise. It may be a tropical park or somewhere that takes your breath away, but wherever it is, this is the beginning. To become emotionally intelligent, you have to be emotionally aware. Close your eyes for a moment in this place that you have chosen and then open them to the splendor of it. What this does is help you to feel very small. Why would you want to feel small? It's actually comforting to know you are just one small piece of the bigger picture. It doesn't make you less important. Imagine a beach without sand. It wouldn't be the same – so each grain of sand plays a part. Thus, this helps you to embrace humility and understand that the world will always be bigger than you are. This helps you to approach life from a humbler perspective and when you can do that, you exercise emotional intelligence at its best. You listen to people. You care about others and you don't put yourself first. That's something that you need to experience because it also helps you to experience a nearness to something you maybe cannot explain. Christians call it God. Others call it their maker. No matter the title you refer to it, it's the acceptance that you are very small and the world around you is huge and diverse.

This helps you considerably, especially if you combine it with your meditation practice. When you meditate you concentrate on the breath? You drop all of the emotions of the moment and breathe. You are in that moment in time. Similarly, when you can do that and are in the habit of doing it daily, it means that you are able to isolate moments that need more attention and recognize those that are merely unimportant events within your day, getting things in better perspective. Remember, I said that you observe thoughts without adding on emotions? Well, meditation encourages that. It helps you to stop filling your mind with clutter that takes away clarity. When you have a clear mind, all of the emotions you feel are positive ones that help you and help the world in which you live. Then, and only then, can you say that you know what emotional intelligence is all about. It's about the silences between the words, the waves that lap up on the shore and the rhythm of your breath. That's all it is and it is forever changing. Don't cling to a moment because very soon that moment is gone. Embrace the new moment with the same enthusiasm that you had when you approached the last moment and if you found that any part of your day was negative, move away from the negativity and find positive solutions.

Self-Esteem and Uncertainties

The moment you have the feeling of lacking sufficient emotional intelligence, you have probably dealt with self-esteem issues and so it's a good idea to up your self-esteem to the extent that you are happy with who you are. Ways of doing this are easier than you may imagine. If you have suffered from other people's criticism in the past, you don't need to lean heavily upon people's approval anymore. Approve of your own actions. Be happy with what you do and if you can manage that, it helps considerably. Here are some exercises that you can do to improve your self-esteem:

Get Rid of Negativity

Be very aware that emotional negativity is not your friend. It doesn't help you and can only hold you back from being the best person you can be. Thus, when you feel negative during the course of the next day or so, write down what made you feel negative and try to come up with a reaction that is positive to take its place. For example, a work colleague said something unkind to you. Write it down. Then think about potential solutions. However, be very aware that the negativity started when your colleague said something that upset you. Thus, it didn't start with you. It started with your reaction. From this, you should learn two things:

- Things only become negative when you allow them to be.

- You should feel empathy toward people who rely upon negativity in their interactions with others.

The emotionally intelligent way to deal with a situation that makes you feel out of place or unhappy is to assess the situation and try to respond to everything that happens in your day in a positive manner. If you get feedback from someone at work that seems negative, thank the person for their feedback and then decide what you can do with the feedback. If it's true what was said, the intelligent way to deal with it is to try to improve. If it's unjust, then you can disregard the problem because your emotional response to it will be noted by the person who tried to make you negative. If it doesn't have any effect, it's likely that they will stop being negative.

Boost Your Self-Esteem

It is an easy task to undertake and one a lot of people don't think about. Give something to someone without expecting any thanks or any kind of reward. That doesn't mean a physical thing. This means some action on your part that is totally volunteered. You may bake a cake for a neighbor. You may give a friend something that you made. You may even volunteer your time to a good cause. Walking your dogs at the local shelter is one area that would be a good one because you are not about what other people think. You are all about how YOU see yourself. You should not be so egoistic as to believe you are better than everyone, but neither should you feel that others are more entitled than you are.

Volunteering helps you to find the balance but only if the volunteering is purposeful, rather than allowing people to exploit your generosity, or using you as a doormat. If you do that in your life, it diminishes your emotional intelligence because these are the kind of people who make you feel less respected or less valuable and that brings out all of the negative emotions.

Self-Management of Your Emotions

There may have been events in your life that bring emotions to the forefront. No-one can change what has happened in the past. However, if you start to manage your emotions and step into the NOW, you can make yourself a much better person. Let me show you how. Eleanor is a young woman who is very pretty. Her boyfriend dumped her and she feels ugly. Whenever she thinks of him, she gets sad and is very negative about life. She feels that the whole situation was her fault. Now, the way that an emotionally intelligent person deals with rejection of this manner is to ask what you can do to protect yourself from that kind of hurt in the future. It's a challenge when there are many negative feelings inside you, but by using mindfulness, you can control those feelings. This implies that every time you feel negative toward life or someone in particular, you drag all of your senses into this moment in time. Past events have gone. There's nothing you can do to change them, but dragging them with you into each day isn't going to help you in your life. Mindfulness is breathing in the moment and accepting what IS rather than what HAS BEEN or COULD HAVE BEEN.

Try this for a moment. Sit very still and let go of your present thoughts, replacing them with this moment in time. Observe everything around you and allow your senses to be in the moment. What is the atmosphere? What's the weather like? What's the aroma you can smell? What can you taste? You have to take control of your emotions and let them know that you are not prepared to be dragged into the retrospective point of view. That moment is gone and now you are in another moment. Make the most of that moment. Treat yourself to something you enjoy. A cup of coffee and peaceful thoughts will help you to get back on track and if you do that each day of your life, you distance yourself from the negativity that was holding your emotional intelligence back in the first place. Now give yourself some positive affirmations to say to yourself each morning, so that you can read them in your journal and start the day on a positive note.

Chapter 5:
The Need to Manage Emotions

Mastering Your Emotions

Emotional intelligence is all about understanding your emotions and the emotions of others and turning them to beneficial use, like enhancing your thoughts. Therefore, in order to have more emotional intelligence, you need to develop ways of mastering your emotions. If you can master your emotions effectively, the journey to emotional intelligence will be easy.

Controlling your emotions doesn't mean repressing or ignoring them. On the contrary, mastering and controlling your emotions means learning to process them and respond to them in a helpful and healthy way. Let's analyze 10 universal emotions that most of us tend to experience throughout our lives. We will be investigating how we can master these emotions.

Discomfort

This uncomfortable emotion usually leads to impatience, boredom, and embarrassment. Discomfort comes when you interpret a set of circumstances or situation in a specific way. Therefore, if you get to change and transform your interpretations of the situation, you will gain control over your emotional experience.

If you want to master this emotion, start by determining what you are doing. Secondly, determine how you are interpreting your experience of the reality. Try taking a different approach if you are not satisfied with the results of what you are doing. For instance, if you are bored by what you are doing, try to do something else with your time. Let your approach employ some flexibility in order to master this emotion.

Fear

This debilitating emotion can leave you anxious, worried, and indecisive. Fear results from an emotional response of what might occur in the future, especially if you take specific action or make a specific decision. Fear can stop you from achieving your objectives and goals. The first step to overcome fear is to separate the 'real' from the 'imagined.' Most fear is based on imagined things that may occur in future.

Our fear mostly comes from lack of knowledge and lack of adequate preparation. Therefore, if you want to manage your fear more effectively, you must first clarify what you really want. Secondly, you must prepare thoroughly for actions you ought to take to achieve your desired outcomes.

Hurt

Hurt makes you feel powerless and leaves you with a sense of loss and jealousy. You may feel hurt due to failure of communicating your needs to others effectively. Therefore, start communicating what you want from your relationships today in a clear and non-threatening manner. If this doesn't work for you, you can evaluate your expectations. Maybe your expectations are not reasonable, have changed over time or they are simply no longer applicable in your current relationship.

Anger

This can spin you out of control emotionally and lead to resentfulness. Anger can actually serve you if you get to understand its underlying meaning. It is important if you get to know that anger often arises when others have violated our rules. We end up feeling angry because we no longer feel in control of our situation. You can actually let go of your anger quite quickly, by evaluating your rules. Maybe, they are out of date, unreasonable or too mean to other people.

Guilt

This emotion leaves you deflated and it can lead to regret. You experience guilt because of your interpretation of what you failed to do, and your view of the exact impact it had on other people. The actual impact your actions could have been quite different than what you guessed them to be.

You can change this by interpreting circumstances and events in your life in a new and unique way to make peace with yourself. If you manage to do so, your guilt will turn into something that can motivate you and empower you to take positive actions.

Frustration

Frustrations occur when you are trying to do something, but you are not getting the desired results. It looks like being held back by some inside force that you cannot control. You can take charge of this feeling by thinking of new possibilities, ideas and other possible solutions to your situation. Look for new information that will provide you with new insight on what you are trying to accomplish.

Try changing your approach or take a look at the issue you're facing from a different angle. Determination, curiosity and a flexible approach will get you there.

Inadequacy

Inadequacy makes you feel unworthy, miserable and incompetent. You are probably experiencing this because you don't have the necessary knowledge, experience and skills to live up to your own high expectations. You may decide to either change the expectations you have for yourself or go out and gain the necessary skills and knowledge to meet your expectations.

You may also experience inadequacy because you undermine your own capabilities. You can ask your friends about their perspective concerning your abilities. You might be surprised at what you hear.

Improving your level of confidence is another way to control this emotion. Self-confidence will help greatly when trying to control any emotion.

Overwhelm

This emotion makes you feel out-of-control and unable to respond to what you're experiencing in a logical and rational manner. What you need is to get back the control, but trying to do it all at once is not a very realistic approach.

You will need to take back the control in small chunks. Take part of your life and divide it into small manageable chunks that you can successfully work with. Let go of any unnecessary commitments and obligations that are weighing you down and take it one chunk at a time.

Disappointment

Disappointment is the emotion that leaves you with a sense of defeat; you didn't achieve the desired result you were working towards.

Handle disappointment by learning from that experience, so that you can better yourself in the future. Look for opportunities that may arise from your disappointment. Change the way you view the experience into a positive one. Instead of thinking you failed because you didn't meet your expectations, think that you just found a way it didn't work and try again.

You can also avoid disappointment by lowering your expectations which will increase the likelihood of them being met. Additionally, evaluate and adjust your goals in order to make them attainable.

Chapter 6:
Self-Motivation to Thrive

It is not enough to just recognize your various emotional states and the implicit role that they play in your life. People who are emotionally intelligent must be able to take control of their emotions and regulate them. Motivation is another critical part of emotional intelligence that must be honed, as your own self-talk and your beliefs about yourself have a direct impact on your motivation and the things that you achieve in life.

Self-Regulation

Self-regulation is about understanding the connection between your thoughts, emotions, and actions and how to hijack this process to help you stay in control. Experiencing emotion as you go through your day is not only natural but a major element of the human experience. By learning to regulate these emotions, however, you can stay in control during strong emotional periods.

Taking Control of Your Emotions

Earlier, we talked about how the subconscious mind perceives the world around us as well as the internal state of our body and mind, that triggers an emotional state. After an emotion is triggered, thoughts and actions follow. By understanding this process, you can take control of your own emotions at critical steps in the process.

You have little control over the emotions that you are experiencing, especially since most result from our previous experiences through the interaction with our surrounding. Instead of trying to control emotions, it is easier to hijack the process between thoughts and actions. You can take control of your thoughts by consciously sending the information that you want to communicate with your mind. Then, these conscious thoughts can change your behaviors.

For example, someone who is going through a break-up after several years may be devastated the first week or so, feeling so distraught that it becomes difficult to focus on work and carry out basic day-to-day tasks like cooking food or taking a shower. The overwhelming sadness is a natural response, but being upset is not a productive emotion. In this scenario, this person might take back control of their emotions by consciously thinking the following:

Feeling sad is a natural response, but it does not contribute to me reaching my goals. I am going to take the energy I would have used on crying and apply it to making positive change in my life. Instead of crying over the relationship, I will accept that it is over and focus on myself. I will use this time to excel at work and cultivate deeper relationships with my friends and family.

By taking over your conscious thoughts, you give yourself the opportunity to control your experience. You have validated your emotions but made the conscious decision to set these emotions aside and continue looking toward the future.

Make Weighted Decisions

Another part of self-regulation is using emotion appropriately during the decision-making process. Weighing your decisions involves being aware of the emotional and logical aspects and how each effect the situation. When you have to make a major decision, create a list of pros and cons. As you list each factor that must be considered, think about the weight that it has on the overall decision.

For example, imagine that you are a surgeon considering a position at one of the most prestigious hospitals — but you have to move to a different country to do it. If you are married or are in a long-term relationship, you may have to consider your partner's wishes if you want to preserve the relationship. If you have only been seeing someone casually for a few months, breaking off the relationship may seem the obvious choice. They do not have as much of an impact on your decision as someone you have a long-term relationship with.

You can practice this skill by visualizing different scenarios in your head where you have to make two decisions. Consider the pros and cons, and then identify which aspects of the decision have the most weight. You can also do this for fictional scenarios with fictional characters — this will give you some insight into the way that other people may make decisions as well.

Plan to Stay in Control

Instead of waiting until you feel a particularly strong emotion to try and exercise control over it, take the time to learn about your triggers. Your emotion journal can help you with identifying the strongest emotions that you experience. Think about some times that you have felt this emotion and what caused it. For example, you might be a level-headed person that becomes angry when you feel that people are ignoring you or when injustice is happening and people are turning a blind eye. Even though being angry about injustice is a natural response, the energy that you feel is better spent trying to fight against injustice or spread awareness.

As you identify situations where your emotions were triggered, write down what caused them. Then, write down what you can do next time instead. For example, imagine that you have seen some news that has made you upset. This might be the death of children in a foreign country or starvation. When you are angered by injustice, a good plan might be, "Take a deep breath. Is there anything I can do at this moment to change it? If not then I should make a mental note of the issue and revisit it later." Some good options for fighting injustice involve making donations to organizations that help or spreading information to people who may not know what is going on.

By having a written plan, you have a clear idea of what to do next time you are upset by injustice. This allows you to respond in a positive way instead of reacting with anger and taking it out on the people that you interact with throughout the day.

Practice Stress Management

Stress management is a major issue for some people especially when they allow situations to take an emotional toll on them. By learning to manage stress, you reduce health problems and increase your longevity. A major part of stress management is having emotional intelligence because your EI gives you insight into what is wrong and how to fix it. Through solving conflict and your ability to identify the source of your stress, you can come up with a creative solution that reduces levels of stress.

In addition to addressing specific causes of stress, it can be useful to promote a bodily environment where it is easier to improve your emotional intelligence. Some of the following habits can ensure that your mind is in the best possible state to use your EQ skills to improve the stress levels in your life:

- Getting 7-8 hours of sleep each night

- Finding time to exercise

- Having fun outside of work

- Spending time alone to recharge

- Choosing foods and drinks that nourish you

- Practice meditation or breathing exercises regularly

- Laugh more often

- Find a good balance between home, work, and a social life

Motivation

One of the biggest problems that people face when they want to achieve something in life is finding the motivation to do it. It is easy to continue putting your goals off until 'later.' Have you ever tried to quit smoking or go on a diet? It is all too easy to say that you will quit after 'just one more' cigarette or start your diet 'in the morning.' Without the motivation to actually do these things, however, they continue to be postponed.

As you increase your emotional intelligence, you will find yourself with a greater sense of motivation and purpose than you might have not experienced previously. Emotional intelligence gives you the confidence that you need to maintain motivation when you are facing obstacles.

A good way to help yourself develop motivation is to look toward the future. Make goals for yourself and get into the habit of doing at least one thing each day that sets you a step closer to your goal, even if it is something small. For example, someone who hates their job might start assembling their resume or do research on different careers they might be interested in. Someone who has the goal of starting a family one day might compile a list of traits that they want in the perfect partner or bring up the subject with their existing partner.

Motivation is a habit that can be slid into as easily as procrastination. By continuing to work toward your goals, you are instilling a sense of confidence in yourself that will help you overcome obstacles to your success. Additionally, you will give yourself that critical forward motion that is necessary if you want to achieve great things in life.

You understand your character more than anyone else does, but you would be wise to ask a good friend what that friend feels you lack emotionally. Tell them that you are trying to become more emotionally intelligent and that you want their help to pinpoint your own weaknesses. The reason I say this is because people who are close to you observe your reactions more than you do. They see you worry and fret over things and they will be able to pinpoint your weaknesses such as:

- Do I worry too much about what people say to me?

- Do I avoid doing things because I am emotionally afraid of failure?

- Do you see me as someone who lets their emotions get in the way of making decisions?

- Do I listen to others enough?

- Am I emotionally ruled by others?

- Am I easy to manipulate?

- Do I ask for people's approval all the time?

Asking your friend these questions, note down the areas where they feel you lack skills and don't take it personally. A good friend wants the best for you and will be able to pinpoint where you could use a little help. It's good to have another individual observe your reactions to others and good friends can really help in this regard.

There are several explanations to why you may react negatively to certain discipline, or why you fight all the time within your mind, rather than accept who you are and what your position in life is. Perhaps you have experienced the busy mind and sometimes ask people to repeat what they said because your mind is too filled up with emotional jumble.

The first exercise that I want you to do is to use something that is used in Buddhism. It's an extremely useful tool and helps to calm the mind, but also helps to change the way that you view life and your interactions with others. It helps you to become calmer by nature and be aware of people around you, which will, in turn, improve your emotional intelligence.

Breathing

I want you to sit somewhere where you are comfortable and where your back is straight. Now, I want you to start to breathe in the manner explained so that you become calmer.

- Breathe in via your nose as you count to eight.

- Breathe out to the count of ten.

While you are doing this, I want you to try and clear all thoughts from your head. Of course, it won't happen straight away because your mind is filled with stuff and it's natural that this should take a little time to tackle. However, breathe in, breathe out and concentrate all your attention on your breathing. This is all there is to basic meditation, but you need to do it for 20 minutes in the morning before you go to work and before your breakfast. What you are doing is giving your mind a little space so that you can see situations with more clarity. When a thought comes to your mind, do not judge it. Imagine it as a picture that you see and then it is gone. The whole point of the exercise is that you learn to be neutral in your approach to your thoughts. Instead of judging things, you simply see it and then it's gone. If you don't distort life by letting your emotions take over each thought that you have, you instantly free up your subconscious mind to finding more intelligent solutions to your problems.

You won't find that this will happen straight away, so keep at it and make this meditative breathing part of your daily routine. It will slow down your heartbeat and your blood pressure and can be made use of during the day if you feel that the world is getting too chaotic for you to deal with. It helps you to build energy within yourself and your posture is also important because you are feeding the inner energy points of your body at the same time.

Keep this practice up and what you will find is that you are not quite so quick to retort to life in a negative fashion. You change your perception and start seeing the bigger picture and are able to control your emotions when it comes to dealing with people. That's a huge boost to your morale because it means that you are more in control of your life and thus more likely to gain promotion and be able to deal with people in a more mature manner. That's what bosses are looking for when they go to promote people and emotional intelligence is important to your welfare too as it stops you from feeling stressed out. Instead of stressing, breathe. Give yourself space to resolve problems rather than letting automatic retort kick in.

Chapter 7:
Learn to Understand Others and Develop Empathy

Empathy is a trait anyone can easily learn and to some extent we all practice empathy in varying degrees as we interact with each other. But showing empathy and being an empath are actually not identical.

Here's how to process the difference between the two.

Imagine you are sitting down at Starbucks with two of your friends that you very much adore. Both are strong in character and while different in personalities, you know they both have big hearts.

Suddenly a couple sitting next to you causes a scene. The guy bangs the table in anger, spilling a perfectly wonderful Frappuccino all over and yells a few words before stomping out. The woman left behind feels utterly crushed and embarrassed. Tears stream down her red cheeks and she hangs her head as low as possible as she quickly tries to clean up the mess created. For a moment, all eyes are on her and you could literally feel everything that she felt.

One of your friends turns to you and asks, "Should we go over there and see if we can help?" As you look over to your friend you notice her cheeks are flushed and her eyes are just as teary as yours. It's almost as if you're both experiencing what the couple experienced. Before you can even respond, your other friend jumps in and says, "Na, she'll be fine. Look she's already stopped crying. Let it go."

What just happened in that scenario?

One of your friends did show some empathy and recognized the discomfort of the woman but that's as far as it went. She was glad to just get on with her day as if nothing happened. The other friend, however, seemed to have had a completely different experience. Her entire body chemistry changed and you felt it too, didn't you?

This is the subtle difference between showing empathy and being an empath.

Empathy is the ability to understand and share the feelings of another. With a little conscious effort, every human being has the ability to demonstrate empathy when the situation calls for it.

When one is an empath, however, it's an entirely different experience. It's more like having an elevated gift and an ability to step into another person's shoes. An empath has the power to step outside his or her own experience and understand what another person is saying, thinking, and feeling. It's more than just being a highly sensitive person and it goes beyond sensing emotions.

According to science, empaths are highly sensitive and can process emotions faster and more intimately. The common acronym for this is HSP meaning a Highly Sensitive Person. A highly sensitive person isn't to be confused with an attention seeker or overly sensitive people who enjoy unpleasant tantrum infused behaviors. It means you are high in sensory processing sensitivity. A true HSP is usually very aware of the feelings of others and very reluctant to cause a scene.

So, from the example I shared of your two friends, one of them does demonstrate empathy, which is great. But the other friend is more likely to be considered an empath.

A true empath goes beyond being an HSP; he or she also has empathic abilities which, when mastered, result in a very powerful being, capable of various things such as healing others.

The natural question that follows is: how does one know whether they possess empathic abilities or not?

I mean, do you actually know if you're an empath? How about we finally shed some light on that.

Here's the Most Important Thing to Always Remember:

When you realize there's a pattern in your life where certain people, situations or triggers result in physical discomfort that cannot be medically diagnosed, know that you're not imagining things or going crazy. You are simply a highly sensitive person with a gift that must be developed, nurtured and successfully managed.

The whole purpose of learning to embrace your empathic abilities and becoming a true empath is so that you can stop being at the mercy of other people's pain, stresses, and conflicts.

Highly sensitive people absorb anything and everything and often they have no control over it. A true empath has mastered his or her abilities and doesn't automatically get overwhelmed by the emotions of another. This is how I've personally redefined for myself what it means to be an empath. How are you going to redefine it for yourself?

If you are truly ready to gain mastery over your special abilities, then it's time to equip yourself with simple living strategies that will empower and help you center yourself so you can finally stop absorbing other people's dysfunctions.

1. Use the Power of Your Breath
First, you need to realize the power contained in your breathing. Whenever you suspect you're picking up someone else's symptoms, bring all your focused attention to your breath for a few minutes. Surrender to this simple act of breathing deeply in and out. Use it to ground yourself and connect to your power.

2. Name It to Tame It

Next, ask yourself, "what is this emotional or physical distress I am feeling?" Whenever we put a label on something, we decrease the momentum of the impact, which gives us ample time to constructively handle the issue.

3. Evaluate it 'in the moment'

Once you've brought it to the forefront of your mind, evaluate this emotion. Don't let this slide and take over your mind and body. Deal with it immediately before it grows into a monster.

Is the distress really yours or have you picked it up from something or someone? Sometimes the answer is both. If for example you're feeling deep fear and it's yours, gently confront what's causing it. You can do this either on your own or by getting professional help. If, however, you realize it isn't yours, pinpoint the obvious generator and work on releasing it.

4. Take a Step Back

This can be physically moving away so you can get into a mindful space to handle the situation or it can be a mental movement. Either way, you want to be able to create some movement that allows you to start reaching for that sense of relief that's absolutely essential in releasing unwanted energies.

5. Become More Aware of Your Mind-Body Connection

Keep breathing deeply. Seek to find where in your body you feel most vulnerable. Chances are if you can find that spot where the alarm is going off you can quickly turn things around and step back into your power. The more you practice this exercise, the better you'll know how your body works.

For example, in my case, my solar plexus is where I go first because I know my tummy is always the first place my alarm hits. By the time I start feeling it on my left shoulder I know it's reached stage two which means the issue is more serious and I need to do something fast.

The physical sensations may not be identical but the same rule will be true for you. Our bodies are such wonderful communicators. Get to understand the signals they send.

So, let's suppose for you it's a migraine headache or a sore throat, the moment you become aware of these symptoms, sit in silence, re-lax your entire mind and body. Practice your deep breathing. Set your palm on the area and practice soothing yourself, giving yourself self-healing. Keep doing it and speaking with yourself until the discomfort dissipates.

If you've been battling with depression, panic attacks or chronic pain for a long time, this simple method when done daily with intention will strengthen and comfort you. It's a great way to reconnect your mind and body and imbue yourself with that feeling of safety that we all need. You are the only one who can heal yourself better. Learn to trust that.

Chapter 8:
Handling Relationships for Success

The people around you may be strangers. They may be people with emotional problems or they may be perfectly happy people. How they feel isn't part of the issue here. What I want you to do today is to learn to be an active listener and stop yourself from voicing your opinion too quickly. Active listening helps you to be empathetic. That means you can put yourself into the shoes of others and imagine what is driving them. When you are able to do that, your interactions with others will be a lot more positive.

Start the day by greeting people in a positive way. Even a smile to a stranger on the street can make a whole heap of difference to the way you approach your day. If you feel negative about sitting in traffic too long, use the time to do something you enjoy. Perhaps you can listen to an audiobook that you don't have time to read. Make the event an enjoyable one. Use music or indulge in learning while you make your way to work. What this does is improve your state of mind, but it also helps you because learning something is positive. You are heading toward an achievement so that's got to be a lot more positive than honking your horn and making everyone around you feel as miserable as you do.

Active Listening

When people speak, they generally talk about themselves. It's not that they think themselves important enough to be the topic of conversation. It's merely because it's what they know about. Thus, you may get involved in all kinds of conversations during the course of the day. You may be fed up with listening to a colleague telling you about her dogs. You may not really want to listen to someone telling you about their love life, but stop for a moment. Why are these people talking to you about things like that? The fact is that a relationship is made up of trust. These people feel that they can trust you enough to discuss their feelings. That's a huge compliment. Thus, instead of nodding and not really listening, learn to be a little more empathetic. If you don't like the subject of dogs, turn the conversation around, but listen to the conversation because to that person, the dog may be the only form of comfort that she has. Active listening means letting others have their say without butting in. It means understanding people's need to get their feelings out in the open. It doesn't mean that you have to take on the world's problems, but it helps you to pass a congenial moment with someone and give them the same amount of attention that you expect to get when you talk to people.

This carefulness also teaches you a lot about your level of empathy because emotionally intelligent people have a high level of empathy.

They know how to steer a conversation. They understand the secrets of making other people feel better than they do at this moment and when you start to do that, the reactions you get from others will be more positive.

What You Say to Others

Remember that what you say to others says a lot about you. The emotions to avoid when you are talking to people are the following:

- Anger

- Indignation

- Jealousy

- Greed

- Selfishness

If you happen to be doing any of the above, put a stop to it. Jennifer was jealous of her sister Jane. Jane got all of the attention of their parents. Jennifer grew up with this bias against her sister, but her sister had done nothing to deserve it. It was their parents who had lavished more attention on Jane than on Jennifer so if anyone was to blame, it would have been the parents. When you carry baggage with you that is negative, it spoils every chance you have at happiness. In the case of Jennifer, she wasted a potential 20 years of friendship with her sister on a mistaken belief that it was her sister's fault that the parents preferred her. When they eventually did make friends, Jennifer saw things from her sister's perspective. It was hard growing up trying to be this person that her parents were making her out to be. She wasn't allowed to make mistakes. She couldn't have fun in her life because her parents' expectations never allowed it. There are always other perspectives. Emotionally intelligent people will see beyond the veneer and know why others are feeling negative. They will also be able to contribute something that makes negative people feel better about themselves.

You cannot go through your life ignoring negative things. These are in your life for a purpose and when you learn to decipher them correctly, you increase your own emotional intelligence. When a negative thing happens, stand back from it and observe it, learning why it happened and then working out what can be done to make the situation more positive for all concerned. That's what emotionally intelligent people do. It takes a bit of learning, but start today.

Emotionally intelligent people are never afraid to admit that they are wrong and they are also unafraid of saying sorry or of forgiving people. You see, the more you insist on holding onto negative emotions, the more they can distort who you are. Forgiveness is a wonderful tool because when you employ it, you empower yourself. The problem is gone. There are no bad feelings left so try to work out who you should forgive in your life because it will take a whole heap of weight from your shoulders.

To share power, men need to be emotionally available and respect their other half, i.e., Emotionally Intelligent (Brittle, 2015).

Yet only 35% of men ARE Emotionally Intelligent.

It's a conundrum, isn't it?

There have been bona fide studies proving the importance of Emotional Intelligence on interpersonal relationships. In one study, for instance, the participants rated their marital satisfaction higher if they also rated their marital partner higher for Emotional Intelligence. Another study demonstrated anticipated greater satisfaction in relationships with a partner of Emotional Intelligence.

A meta-analysis of six studies with more than 600 participants found a *significant association* 'between EQ and romantic relationship satisfaction and it works both ways. The higher your own Emotional Intelligence, the more satisfied you will be in a romantic relationship, PLUS the higher your partner's EQ, the happier you will also be.

Isn't its worth beefing up your Emotional Intelligence for the pair of you, whether it's for your present or future Mr. or Mrs.?

The good news is that happy couples aren't necessarily better, luckier, richer or more intelligent than the rest of us; they are just in touch with their emotionally intelligent side.

As Dr. John Gottman himself, possibly the world's lead researcher on marriage, says: *"Happily married couples aren't smarter, richer, or more psychologically astute than others. But in their day-to-day lives, they have hit upon a dynamic that keeps their negative thoughts and feelings about each other (which all couples have) from overwhelming their positive ones. They have what I call an emotionally intelligent marriage."* (John Gottman and Nan Silver, 2018)

How does this manifest itself? According to Dr. Gottman, an emotionally intelligent marriage includes two partners who are committed to awareness of themselves and the other, and the ability to manage their own emotional state and its impact on the other partner. So, a classic trait of Emotional Intelligence.

To specify further, he adds: *"In the strongest marriages, husband and wife share a deep sense of meaning. They don't just 'get along' — they also support each other's hopes and aspirations and build a sense of purpose into their lives together."*

If marriage is a journey, you both know why you're in the car together and appreciate where you're going.

It's all the easier to live up to those marriage promises – to love, honor, respect and understand each other – if you are an emotionally intelligent couple. Not only can it help you avoid divorce or relationship breakdown, but as happily married people lead longer and healthier lives, it's great for your health too.

Emotional Intelligence isn't just crucial to love relationships. It's valuable for family and friends too, helping to sustain ongoing positive relationships.

But if you're terrible at EQ, how *can* you improve? How sure can you be that you are providing your significant other, friends and family the support they need?

Most of the time, in close personal relationships, your actions will be natural, and you may not even be aware that you're using your EQ skills. If you're naturally low in Emotional Intelligence, however, it may take more purposeful thought and effort, but remember that EQ skills can be learned.

The truth is that you're more likely to be aware of your EQ skills (or lack thereof) if you don't have them.

Relationships: Does the next section sound like anyone you know, someone close to home perhaps? If you can't recognize them in yourself, has your partner or family complained about you suffering from any of the following? It's probably time to deal with it.

Out of Control Feelings: We all know by now that Emotionally Intelligent people can regulate their emotions. If your EQ needs work, you may be prone to lashing out in anger or giddy happiness for no real reason, or any other OTT emotional reaction.

Poor Friendships: How many close friendships do you have? Most people low in EQ struggle to maintain good relationships with co-workers and friends.

Can't Read Emotion: Do you often find yourself clueless about your partner's emotions, or blindsided by a reaction? You may be unable to read non-verbal cues, such as facial expressions or body language, or struggle to interpret tone of voice. So much of our communication is not said verbally. If you can't interpret that, you will struggle to make an emotional connection because you never quite understand the thoughts of the other person. The good news is that we have a section on non-verbal communication coming up just for you.

Poker Face: Can your partner tell what you're thinking and feeling, or do you have a poker face, unable to express your own emotion?

Are you Emotionally Inappropriate? Do you get angry over nothing, or fail to realize you are angering someone else? Perhaps you are inappropriate, such as telling jokes or laughing at a funeral. These can be signs that you struggle with the social side of emotional expression.

Can't Handle Sadness: Do you prefer to walk away from negative emotions or sadness, struggling to show empathy or support? A lack of empathy signals poor Emotional Intelligence. Do you find emotional movies leave you cold, for instance? Don't be fooled into thinking it's a male versus female thing; it's not. It's very possibly a sign that you have low EQ.

Overplay Logic: Logic has its place in relationships, but if you over-stress logic and cognition over emotions (and typically downplay the latter), it's a sign that you are subconsciously aware of your low EQ and trying to pretend it doesn't matter. Little tip: it does, for all the reasons I mentioned above.

Odd Interpretation of Emotions/Conflicts: Have you been accused of over-reacting or having an odd reaction to conflict or emotions? Perhaps you acted hostile and defensive when there was no need. Often the root cause of this is confusion as opposed to malice, very possibly because of the above. Of course, when people don't under-stand that, you tend to withdraw even more.

Assuming you freely recognize your lack of Emotional Intelligence and appreciate the negative impact it is having on your personal life, what can you do about it? How can you go about developing your EQ in re-lationships in particular?

How to Develop your EQ in Relationships

I've already shared a lot of tips for improving your EQ in general ear-lier in the book. A lot of what I suggested there will help your EQ across the board, including with friends, family and significant other.

Now though I'm going to suggest a couple of further tips specific to romantic relationships. It's worth following even if you haven't found that special someone yet... who knows, perhaps becoming more in tune with your emotional side will help you land them!

Learn to Describe your Emotions

Yes, I know I've mentioned this a couple of times before, but it really is worth developing a strong emotional vocabulary in the context of relationships. Think of how you describe your emotions – happy, sad, angry... anything deeper? If you're sad, for instance, would you ever think of yourself as melancholy, depressed, grief-stricken, ill or nostalgic?

As we know by now, developing a wider emotional vocabulary allows you to go deeper and to correctly label your emotions, which in turn helps you to react accordingly. Having a wider emotional vocabulary encourages you to move past your first initial emotion, say anger, to determine exactly what lies beneath. Often our first instinctive emotional response seems like the most powerful, but it's not always the true story.

Say you have an argument with your wife. You feel and recognize your first emotion, anger. Would you ordinarily stop there? Now that you're seeking a stronger Emotional Intelligence, you should push past the anger to find what you're really feeling – could it be hurt, jealous, anxious, worried, embarrassed, ashamed?

Being hurt, for instance, feels very different from being angry, doesn't it? Or perhaps you're ashamed because you couldn't give your wife what she needed from you? Each emotion carries a different weight and influences how you relate to your partner, helping to make your relationship more genuine. Imagine if you'd just stopped at anger? You would understand a lot less.

Don't forget. While your first emotional reaction may seem the most powerful, it may also be the least honest.

Work on Relationship Awareness

The key to Emotional Intelligence is to be aware of, and in control of, our own emotions, while also recognizing emotions in others. Every single one of us needs something from our significant other, whether it's love, trust, support, affirmation.

Of course, what we need from the other changes as we age, our relationship grows, our circumstances alter etc.

What does your wife or husband need from you? What *'emotional nutrients'* do they need that would feed your relationship? *(If the word 'nutrients' is confusing to you, consider emotional needs instead. What emotional needs does your wife need you to address?)*

Just go ahead and ask. Ask your partner to write down the three most important emotional needs or *'nutrients'* that they have and want from your relationship. Write your own list independently. Swap and discuss how you can make sure the relationship or marriage can meet both lists.

How to Understand Body Language

There's a formula that's often bandied around when we start to talk about body language and non-verbal communication – the 55/38/7 rule (Belludi, 2008). It's a percentage formula that demonstrates how much is communicated when you're NOT speaking. Yes, that's right. People communicate even when they're *not* talking.

The 7% of the formula represents how much of communication is spoken. Your words, no matter how carefully you choose them, only account for 7% of all communication. Both liberating and daunting, isn't it?

In total, so the formula goes:

- 55% of all communication comes from body language

- 38% from tone of voice

- 7% are actual words spoken.

Of course, there has been some dispute with the exact figures and it's fair to point out that such a simple theory can't possibly apply to every situation. But, experts agree, it's a pretty good ballpark and it really does emphasize the importance of body language.

Understanding someone's body language can tell you so much about a person, but what if you just weren't born knowing the cues? What if it all simply passes you by, and you fail to notice your wife is angry despite saying she's not, or your son is lying to you when he promises not to have a party this weekend? Can you learn how to recognize body language?

Let me tell you a little story. I was sat minding my own business in a local coffee shop recently *(meaning I was people watching, fascinated by their interactions)*. A young couple walked in and sat next to me, arguing all the while. I politely tried to ignore them *(okay, not really)* but they made it hard. The argument seemed to stem from the fact that the boyfriend had communicated with an ex-girlfriend, a fact he was trying hard to pretend didn't mean anything. Of course, his body language gave him away.

He tried so hard to convince his girlfriend with logic but was oblivious to what his body language and tone of voice – defensive, mock offended, *'caught like a rabbit in headlights'* – really revealed. Of course, we don't see our own body language so it's often hard to be sure if it's failing our intentions.

His girlfriend, of course, a woman of obvious Emotional Intelligence, saw straight through him, but for some reason either decided to accept his protestations or was saving them up to use against him later. Finally, she calmed down and her hapless and low EQ boyfriend thought that was the end of it. They sat in silence – communicating volumes to anyone who cared to look – and he thought he'd got away with it.

When they left, he tried to seal the deal with a hug. He was happy that she acquiesced, but her body language – stiff as a plank of wood, refusing to make eye contact – should have told him that he really shouldn't touch her.

I tell you, he was so busted. The next time I saw her in the same café, she was alone. I never did ask what happened to the boyfriend, but I can guess.

You see, if you're so blind to body language, you miss out on so much.

What is Body Language?

It's everything from eye contact *(or lack of)*, gestures, facial expressions, posture, space *(do they invade yours?)*, and touch *(a weak handshake versus a bear hug, for example)*.

Did You Know: Facial expressions are universal. They are the same across cultures for happiness, sadness, fear, shock and disgust etc. The same is *NOT* true of other forms of non-verbal communication, such as gestures and body language, so be careful!

Uses of Body Language

According to The Importance of Effective Communication by Edward G. Wertheim, body language can be used to underline or complement a verbal message *(think of a pat on the back when congratulating someone)*, or to repeat what they say wholeheartedly. When it matches the spoken words, it increases trust and rapport between people.

Body language can, and often is, used instead of words – eye contact can communicate much more than words alone, don't you think? It can also contradict what someone is trying to convey with words.

The kicker about that last point – research studies show that if your body language contradicts your spoken word, people are much more likely to believe the former. Not to mention distrust you. If you can read body language well, it's a built-in lie detector.

Body language can't really be faked. Unless you're a master manipulator and 'on' all the time, your true intentions will slip out, whether it's thanks to a gesture, a touch, an eye-roll or some other little clue.

How to Recognize Body Language
There are far more clues to body language than we can possibly talk about in one chapter – entire books have been written on it, after all. However, there are a few steps that you can take to make yourself more open and effective at interpreting non-verbal communication. They include:

Managing Stress

When you're stressed, you are much more likely to miss the non-verbal signs that other people are putting out there. You'll be prone to misreading events and handling personal conversations poorly. Managing stress is important for effective communication. If you're stressed by a discussion, take a time-out. Regain your emotional equilibrium before you say or do something you'll regret. Remember your emotions are contagious, as we talked about above.

Work on Recognizing Your Emotions

Being aware of your and other people's emotions and how they influence you is a fundamental part of Emotional Intelligence and the purpose of this book. It's also a key component of recognizing body language, so there's a bonus!

Look for Inconsistencies

Possibly one of the best tips for reading body language that I can give you is to look for inconsistencies between what someone says and what their non-verbal communication suggests. Ideally it should reinforce their words. If someone is saying yes while shaking their head no, that's something to be wary of, for instance. A word of advice, however – don't try to evaluate every single non-verbal signal that you receive; it will make your head explode. People naturally consider all the clues given during a conversation to gain an overall impression of whether their words, tone of voice and body language are consistent or inconsistent with what is being said.

Pay Attention to Your Instincts

Gut feeling is important, don't dismiss it. If you suspect someone isn't being truthful, you may be subconsciously picking up on a conflict between verbal and nonverbal clues.

If in doubt, ask

If someone's body language seems to contradict their spoken word – and it's not a potentially dangerous situation – feel free to ask for clarification. Don't get frustrated. Say something like, *"You said X and Y, but your body language suggests you think differently. Can you help me to understand?"* Just be careful not to do it aggressively or in an adversarial manner.

Well done on wanting to improve your EQ and your knowledge of body language to strengthen your relationships with your nearest and dearest.

Program Yourself to Become Successful

We all are looking for that mental edge when it comes to achieving what we want. Most often your mind is your worst enemy when it comes to succeeding in life. You should realize that instead of fighting with your mind you can program it to work in your endeavor to reach.

Success is a powerful word, which we all realize is hard to achieve. It takes something extraordinary to reach your goals, but it is still very possible. Alongside a little dedication, programming the human mind to succeed is all it takes. How do you program the mind to succeed in life?

Rid Yourself of Self-Doubt

Success becomes elusive when we give up even before we try. We always keep telling ourselves what we are not. We drive in hard our weaknesses that de-motivate us and prevent us from making effective efforts. A simple way to overcome this roadblock to success is by creating an 'I-Am' list.

Note down all the good qualities that you think you possess on one side of the paper and everything that you want to be on the other side. It keeps you updated with your goals and missions in life at all times. It also boosts your confidence and reminds you of all the great qualities that you possess and would maintain once you succeed in your quest. These outlines are necessary because it is from here that you would draw strength and inspiration to work harder and perform better in life.

Positive Thinking

Positive thinking is a must for you to succeed. Emotionally Intelligent people never see the glass as half empty. They see the glass as half full and do not hesitate one bit to drink it all up when they are thirsty. Positive thinking makes one confident and surer of oneself, promoting ideas that lead you to success. Hence never feel dejected or disenchanted. Rather look for the sunny side up in matters of life. When you want to achieve something in life, it becomes important that you promote that idea in both your thoughts and speech. When you keep thinking just about the hurdles in your way, they appear much bigger. Tell your mind that no matter what it takes, you are unafraid to sweat it out to achieve what is in your mind. Take the course of action required as a means to an end with the end signifying your success.

Meditate to Gain Clarity

It is very common that people lose interest midway through their efforts and their dreams and ambitions never materialize in their lives. Meditation and self-introspection are the ways that prevent individuals from getting disenchanted in their mission. Take out a small amount of time from your busy schedule to ruminate about your actions, thoughts, motivations, desires, and plans. Think about what is preventing you from succeeding and how that hurdle can be overcome. Ponder on your strengths and how you can gain from them in your endeavor to achieve. Mentally prepare yourself for the hard work because there is no skipping that. Meditation helps clear your mind and makes you remain focused and energized while you make efforts to succeed. Our thoughts hold the power that can make us fail or succeed in life. Taking control over your mind is essential for you to succeed and to have once familiarized yourself with your mind there is no stopping you from succeeding in life.

The principle of goal-setting in the management of emotions - before deciding what to do with this or that emotion, one must answer the question, "what do we want as a result?"

'Reframing' is a tool for replacing negative emotions with positive ones.

Rapid methods of neutralizing emotions that impede effectiveness (for example, breathing practices, movement, diet).

Chapter 9:
Leading with Emotional Intelligence in Social Settings

We need to explore how your emotional intelligence can change your life through your social skills. Let's examine how having a strong Emotional Intelligence can change the way you socialize with the people around you. The practices in this section will help you further advance your emotional intelligence in a way that influences you to have more positive interactions with others.

These skills will develop you both inside and outside. This is because it supports you in getting to know yourself even more, which is one of the very foundational parts of being emotionally intelligent. It is also because it will change the way you interact with others and therefore your social circle may change drastically. At the very least, the way you engage with your social circle will change.

Here are the skills you need to begin practicing to empower and enhance your social skills through emotional intelligence.

Be Approachable and Open

Increasing your emotional intelligence is partly about putting down your guard, and letting yourself be approached by other people. When you are emotionally intelligent, you no longer fear being hurt by others because you are capable of recognizing the reality of this hurt and you trust that you can move through it effectively. As such, you are more open.

Practice how to be more open to others. Be willing to let other people approach you, keep your body language open and welcoming, and be kind to those you meet. When you are open and approachable, it becomes easier for you to increase your ability to connect with others. These connections and the relationships you may gain from them can teach you an incredible amount about yourself, who you are, and why you are that way. Relationships and connections with other humans are a great opportunity to learn more about ourselves and to develop ourselves beyond where we have already grown.

Gain Perspective

If you have ever heard the phrase "put yourself in their shoes", then you likely know the importance of being able to see things from someone else's perspective. A great way to develop your emotional intelligence and create stronger relationships is to set the intention to gain perspective. Instead of delaying until an issue arises or having someone else need to point this out for you, gain perspective simply because you are curious. Seek to learn more about how other people view the world around them.

When you intentionally learn more about other people's perspective, and you are willing to see things from their angle without having to be asked, you increase your empathetic abilities. It becomes easier for you to relate to other people, understand their opinions and interpretations of the world around them, and create stronger connections with them. It also helps inspire you to challenge your own beliefs and deepen your understanding of the world around you.

Be Curious About Others

Many individuals struggle to create connections because they do not know how to be curious about other people. As humans, especially when we are on a journey to understanding ourselves, we can find ourselves in a state of self-absorption. We may struggle to connect with others because we seem to lack interest in them. This can lead to us excessively talk about ourselves. This is not only ineffective in creating relationships, but it also stunts your growth.

Being curious about others and asking questions to learn more about them, is a way to deepen our connections, but also a way to create a stronger understanding of ourselves. When we are curious about others, it also turns into a curiosity about ourselves. We begin to learn more about life, ourselves, and others through the relationships we build with other people.

This does not mean that you should only talk about the other person. It merely means that you should consider developing a more even playing field. Ask as much as you share, and be curious as often as you reflect. Focus on creating a communication style that allows you to create a mutual relationship between yourself and others- one where you learn as much as they do and you are both engaged in the connection.

Do Not Be Afraid to Be First

If you are having difficulty being open in relationships, chances are, you have difficulty being the first one to spark a conversation or create a connection as well. If you genuinely want to practice developing your emotional intelligence in a personal setting, take some time to practice being the first person to open conversations and start-up relationships. The world is filled with people who are uncertain about how to approach other people. Social media and the internet brought changes to the way our social skills are developed, which can deeply inhibit our emotional intelligence.

Spending some time learning to open conversations, being open and friendly, and developing relationships with other people are important. This will teach you how to be more charismatic and friendly, but it will also teach you a lot about yourself. You will begin to learn how to approach certain people, which types of engagement are appropriate for each unique setting, and how you can break the ice with different personality types. These practices are a great way to understand yourself deeper and will help you discover what kinds of personalities you get along with the most.

Reduce Time on Social Media

The amount of time that the average person spends on social media is incredibly high. This time may seem harmless to you, but the reality is that it can inhibit your social skills. The way that we communicate online is extremely different from how we communicate in person. If your connections are predominantly online, it can create a challenge for you in learning how to start conversations, carry conversations in the real world, read people in person, and gauge situations. Emotions are not communicated by the internet as easily as they are in person. The internet can be completely void of emotion or can include highlighted feelings or outright lies.

Learning to move your communications to a more face-to-face approach will support you in being able to read other people easier. You will be able to identify what various body languages mean, the 'vibe' of the situation, and additional information that can support you in understanding everything you are interpreting from the other person. Being able to understand and process this information will have a powerful impact on your ability to interpret, experience, and reflect emotions in personal settings.

Practice Your Emotional Intelligence

Like any other skill you may desire to develop in your life, nothing is as powerful as practice. Taking the time to practice your emotional intelligence skills by applying the practices you have learned in this book will significantly increase your emotional intelligence overall.

While consuming content and information, learning through intellect is valuable in supporting your growth, it will only get you so far. The real way to develop emotional intelligence is to apply the practices into your life.

The best way to practice enforcing emotional intelligence in your life and relationships is through choosing a few practices and mastering those before moving on to new ones. Attempting to master too many emotional intelligence practices all at once, will likely result in you feeling confused and overwhelmed. You may struggle to apply anything, increase your stress levels, and reduce your chances of success. Instead, take your time, be patient with yourself, and set realistic goals. Discover which areas you could use the most practice in and focus on starting in these areas. Then, you can begin to expand out to new practices.

Consider developing your emotional intelligence to be a process. This is something you can practice and refine for the rest of your life. The more you take your time and invest in each step, the more you stand to gain from it all. Be realistic and gentle with yourself. Make use of this move to strengthen a personal relationship with the real you.

Network Often

Networking is a great way to develop relationships with other people. When you regularly attend networking events or opportunities, you open yourself up to the opportunity to practice opening up new conversations, connecting with many different personality types, and learning new perspectives. Networking is truly beneficial on so many levels.

The best way to begin practicing networking is to look up local networking events in your area. There are networking events for virtually everything. You can join a networking event about crafting or dogs, one that is related to your career or a specific interest or hobby you have. Starting at events that are relevant to the information you know about or are interested in is a great way to get started. This way, you already know at least one thing you share in common with the other people at the event. Breaking the ice becomes easier, meaning developing your social skills and increasing your emotional intelligence through socializing becomes easier as well.

Pay Attention to Your Tone

Your voice tone when communicating, as well as the way you present yourself in communication, can say a lot. These two levels of communication can result in us sending the right message or the wrong message to the person we are communicating with. When people lack emotional intelligence, their words may be engaged as interested, but their tone of voice and body language may come across as sarcastic, rude, or uninterested. If your words are contradicted by your tone of voice and body language, you are going to struggle to have strong communications with other people.

When you are communicating, practice using a tone of voice that accurately reflects what you are saying. Furthermore, make sure that this tone of voice is natural and does not sound forced. Attempting to manipulate a tone of voice that is not coming out naturally can actually make you seem less approachable and even contradictory. Instead, focus on projecting your true emotions into your voice. This is a wonderful way to infuse your tone of voice naturally with the emotions you are genuinely experiencing; it will help you come across more open and friendly.

In a situation where you are upset or where you disagree with the other person, refrain from projecting too much anger in your voice. This can quickly come off as aggressive and hostile. Focus on keeping your voice even and fair, and use your words to communicate your feelings at this point.

When it comes to body language, you may benefit from reading a book specifically about body language, or otherwise engaging in learning specifically about body language. Body language is a vast form of communication that every human use. It can have a great impact on how you are received by others, whether or not they are consciously aware of these receptions. Furthermore, it can support you in reading others as well. Remember, our bodies say a lot about our emotions. Learning to read others' body language, and to use your body language as a tool for communication, can increase your emotional intelligence and magnify your social skills with others.

Intimacy

When it comes to personal relationships, your feelings and emotions come first. Any idea or feeling when not expressed does not have any value.

Role of EQ in Intimacy

EQ is an ability to understand and act upon others' and one's own feelings or emotions. What has it to do with intimacy? Let us consider a situation; you come home after a long stressful day, and you expect a calm and peaceful night. Your husband or wife is in a terrible mood and needs a person to talk with. He/she is continually trying to talk about the topic you want to avoid. The normal output would be shouting or yelling that you are in a bad mood or cut short the conversation by saying that you are not ready to talk about it now. A person with high EQ would try to shift the topic to a related or less stressful topic. The person may either ask to take a break by taking him or her out for a talk, along with dinner. This would ease off both.

EQ would help to be aware of the emotions at the moment and manage it, in the right way. It also helps to understand other people's emotions and work accordingly. If things don't turn out well, he should be able to be resilient within a very short period, without holding grudges or an ego. He should be able to communicate effectively.

How to express intimacy?

There is no one line answer stating that by doing so, anyone from any part of the world can show intimacy with another person. The ways of expressing intimacy differ from one person to the other. One of my friends touches his partner's nose and wiggles with his nose. However, if I do so, my partner would think that there is something wrong with his nose. For another friend, sitting on the deck with a cup of coffee and talking about all that happened during the day is called intimacy.

In short, intimacy is the way to express that you like them and you are comfortable being with them. This can be expressed in words but, not completely. You should be able to manage your emotions. You should be able to control your anger, force out a real smile or act surprised when she gives you a small gift, to increase intimacy.

Emotions and Intimacy

A friend of mine and his partner went to a club. The club was very crowded as it was New Year's Eve. He was constantly holding her hand and frequently looking into her eyes. This indicates that he is there for her and the staring made her feel comfortable.

There are a lot of differences between a tight hug and a little hug kind of action. The tight hug would mean that you missed her or you do not want to move away from her. A hug like action would say that you have hugged her for the sake of doing so.

Watching his eyes while talking or holding her shoulder while she talks about her rough childhood or smiling to assure that you are there for him/her would all increase the intimacy. Moreover, when it comes to intimacy, managing bad emotions are more essential than expressing positive emotions. For instance, you are angry at him, for a certain reason. You can either spit it out or wait till the moment passes and talk when the air is clear.

What to do When You Were Wrong

The best way is not to blame or to find fault with your partner. For instance, if she is angry that you are not organized, it is not right to pinpoint the things she is not good at. You can;

- Apologize for the time-being even if you are wrongly accused and then talk about it later.

- Let her spill out everything and then ask her ways to help you rectify it.

- If you have a valid point, wait till she completes. Reply in a soft voice. Yelling loud will not prove you are innocent.

- If your partner is deeply hurt, try to cool her off with small gifts or apologetic letters or anything that would make her smile a little.

- Make sure you admit that it's your fault.

What to Do When Your Partner Does Something Wrong?

Remember not to take advantage of the situation just because your partner has committed a mistake. When your partner is wrong;

- Talk to him/her and explain what's bothering you. Explain what can be done and how much you are willing to adjust.

- If your partner is not ready to listen, wait till the moment has passed and talk about it another time when you are both in a good mood.

Even if after continuous explanation your partner is not ready to rectify, there are two options: one is to live with it and the second is to explain how much you are affected by it and what would happen if the process continues.

Fighting and name calling will not solve any problem without causing a lot more to deal with. Remember people make mistakes and they tend to make the same mistake more than once. Just because they committed the same mistake after you explained all the points, does not mean that they ignore you. When they are afraid or sorry for making the mistake, it indicates that they care about you and do not want you to get hurt by any means.

Chapter 10:
How to Handle Conflicts the Right Way

Another aspect of strong social skills is the ability to manage conflict, both at home and in the workplace. Conflict can often seem to come out of thin air can't it, and if you're one of those people who prefers to ignore it, well, stop! Let's face it most conflict doesn't miraculously go away. It festers and grows until something breaks, often relationships.

A good conflict manager will bring the disagreement out into the open, encourage the sharing of emotions and open discussion, reduce any hidden issues, aid both parties in recognizing each other's feelings and encourage them to recognize logical positions. They will try to seek win-win solutions, where both parties feel they have earned something from the exchange.

Tips for Handling Conflict

Probably the easiest model for handling conflict is the straightforward model below:

Describe the Situation, Express Your Feelings, Ask for What You Would Like Done

A couple of quick pointers:

If you're an active participant in the disagreement, take the time to cool down before tackling the problem. Vent if you need to, rant too, talk to a friend, but identify and deal with your emotions first. If someone around you is heated, take the time to calm them down first. Do this before you email your boss back or remind your significant other that you care for them before complaining about something.

Address the problem when you are both calm. The first thing you should do is to identify what the conflict is and make sure you and the other person (or the interested parties, if you're the mediator) agree on what the problem is. This is where describing the situation in our model above comes in. You'd be amazed how many times two people in a conflict can disagree on the cause or the problems arising from it.

Ideally, propose solutions that are mutually beneficial (the win-win I talked about earlier) and be sympathetic if the other person is unwilling to concede certain things (though stand firm on your own issues too).

Try to end on a co-operative note, even if you can't agree on all points. Demonstrate to your boss or co-worker, for instance, that you want to work towards the same goal even if you disagree on how to get there. Let your wife, husband or significant other know that you will try to work on the issues he or she has raised even if you can't agree to them all. Relationships, whether at home or in business, work best when the people involved believe they are on the same page, with the aim of achieving the same goals.

I followed the model above with two of my team when conflicts arose at work. Both seemed to get on okay while I was in the office, but when I left – and my second-in-command deputized for me – communication and teamwork broke down. Both complained about the other, yet I knew that both were at the top of their game, so what happened when I was out of the office?

The first time it occurred I dealt with it independently, speaking to the two of them separately, but it happened again. Soon both started sniping at each other, and I knew I couldn't allow it to go on any further. I worked off-site at our second site a lot and relied on Mark to keep the team productive in my absence.

I called a meeting with the pair of them, warning them ahead of time that we were going to deal with the conflict professionally and calmly, with no raised voices.

I set out the game plan from the start. Victoria, the most junior, would go first as she was the one who effectively had the complaint, which was the way she was treated by my deputy when I wasn't in the room. She would have the opportunity to explain the situation and the conflict as she saw it and express her feelings, plus to say what she would like to see done differently. I made the point again that no-one would be attacked, and we would deal with the disagreement calmly.

I also made sure to tell Mark, my deputy, in front of Victoria, that he should listen to Victoria, consider if he agreed with the situation as she laid it out, and if not, to express his own view of the problem calmly and again without attacking. I stressed that he should apologize only if he felt he had done something wrong, but that he shouldn't be defensive and should be open to co-operation.

Victoria described the situation as she saw it. Effectively, it came down to Mark being overzealous with his deputy role, 'bossing' the team about unnecessarily, but also in part doing the job that he was hired to do. (The team were about to move to a different position in the media empire we worked in, and Mark had been employed to get them ready for a faster-more paced pressured role).

Mark listened to Victoria's complaints and was genuinely stunned by some of the examples that she gave of his behavior. Giving Mark props, he admitted he hadn't realized that some of his actions could be construed in the way that they had and he apologized for making Victoria feel that she couldn't be trusted with her work. That had never been his intention.

As per my instructions, however, he refused to apologize for being 'tough' on the team and pushing them to do better, pointing out that was why he was brought in. To do the hard job when I couldn't be in the office. As a mediator, I explained his role to Victoria more fully.

Victoria listened and appreciated the distinction but did point out that Mark was like two different people – when he was deputizing and when he wasn't. The conflict confused the team, and they never knew 'which' Mark they were getting. The jovial Mark who liked to joke and be one of the team, or the buttoned-up 'boss' Mark who micromanaged and never felt like anything was good enough.

Mark, of course, hadn't realized he acted any differently during those moments in charge and I hadn't been around to see them. Faced with specific examples from Victoria, however, he accepted the point was well made and pledged to find a happier, common ground. He was open to change but assertive enough to point out that he was still in charge when deputizing and wouldn't apologize for pushing the team when he felt it was needed.

Victoria respected that, and indeed I could see her respect for Mark grow from that day on. She left the meeting happy that she had been listened to.

Subsequently, Mark and I worked on his issues, specifically his confusion over his role when I was and wasn't in the office. When I was there to lead the team, for instance, where did he stand? We helped him to find a position of authority that didn't ebb and flow according to the situation each day.

Mark and Victoria never had any issues after that; in fact, they became close friends. That meeting, while challenging as a mediator and even more daunting as a participant, was the best conflict management tool we could have used.

The idea in any conflict management situation is to be assertive without being aggressive. Indeed, assertiveness is probably the most important skill in conflict management. Active listening is also crucial to ensure you understand the positions of those involved in the conflict, whether you are the mediator or an active participant.

You will need the ability to recognize emotions in others (and ideally be able to point out to others when the emotions are okay to express or when they are inappropriate. Empathy is also an extremely beneficial skill.

Be aware of the way you solve a conflict in your personal life and at work. When conflict resolution seems like a tedious, hostile, or unpleasant situation, it shows that the techniques being used are ineffective. The best thing that you can do if you are struggling with conflict resolution is to set aside time to practice. Below, you'll find some techniques that you can use to help solve conflicts in a positive way.

Solve Imaginary Conflicts

Think of scenarios, either real-life or made-up and try to come up with a solution. Write down the problem, as well as the needs of all the parties involved. Then, try to come up with a solution that fulfills the needs of all parties involved. Practice explaining this situation as you would when speaking to someone who is potentially upset. Explain your point and emphasize that you have taken their needs into clarification. If they are dissatisfied, re-evaluate the solution or ask more about the other person's specific needs so you can reach a solution that appeases all parties. As you continue to practice and become more aware of the emotions of yourself and the people around you, conflict resolution and problem-solving will become significantly easier.

As you solve conflicts in your personal relationships, you will find that healthy, constructive relationships bring you closer to the other person instead of pushing you away. By positively resolving conflict, it shows that you trust the other party enough to let them be an active part of the conflict resolution process. When solutions are reached without either party being punished, threatened, manipulated, or neglected in some way, it brings about a sense of safety and creativity. In a work environment, you will be seen as someone who prioritizes finding a solution and people may turn to you for advice, as you are capable of rationally viewing all sides of the situation before coming up with a solution.

Describe Problems and Conflicts Using 'I' Statements

'I' statements are designed to help other people understand how you are feeling. They are designed to be non-threatening and open up the channels of communication. Rather than assigning blame, using 'I' statements allow you to describe your personal impact as a result of the problem. It is a way to communicate what you are feeling without assuming the other person has intentionally hurt you.

The basic template that you can use to form an 'I' statement is '"I feel... when you... because..." This identifies the problem clearly, as well as the reason that you are impacted by it. Imagine that your spouse is a bartender and it upsets you. Instead of continuing to feel negative emotions like insecurity and anger each time that they go to work, a better approach is to address the issue. You might say, "I feel upset when you flirt with people at work because it makes me feel like you are not committed to our relationship." This formula assigns blame where it belongs—on their position as a bartender and your insecurity in the relationship. Instead of feeling like you are accusing them or blaming them, they may reassure you of their commitment or explain their reasoning for flirting. This opens up both sides of the discussion and allows both of you to share, which is a wonderful place to begin at when you are trying to reach a compromise.

Solving Conflict in the Workplace

Part of using emotional intelligence in the workplace is exhibiting your leadership skills and your ability to resolve conflicts. Many of the skills addressed earlier can also benefit the way you interact with people in the workplace. By learning to read the emotions of people around you, you can effectively manage people in a work environment.

You can also learn how to communicate your needs more effectively in a way that encourages people to do what you want.

Even when people work well together, the work environment can bring about competitiveness as people want to stand out. When working in groups, this desire to shine and the difficulty in admitting flaws can make group work difficult. As a rational thinker, you have better insight to lead the group to a collaborative solution. For example, you might have everyone write their ideas down. Then, each of them can be presented and discussed in turn. At the end of the discussion, the best idea can be chosen and altered to fit the group's needs, or a few different ideas can be combined.

Be Clear When Communicating Your Needs

One of the biggest obstacles to a seamlessly flowing workplace is miscommunication. When managers and employees are not clear about the things that they need, it leads to disappointing results that reduce morale. Instead of leaving things to chance, be clear about the things that you need. You might find that it is better to use e-mail for communication than spoken word since it serves as a record of what is required. You can also encourage people to question you when they do not understand. Not only does this invite collaboration and help employees get the task done right the first time, but it also clarifies areas of communication where you may still be struggling.

Find the Right Attitudes about Conflict

People who avoid conflict may have bad experiences with disagreements in the past or they might worry about maintaining a healthy relationship after conflict. However, conflict is inevitable — no two people will have the same needs, desires, and goals at every moment of their life. Having the right attitude toward conflict means having a confident mindset when it comes to finding a solution. As you develop your emotional intelligence skills, you will find that you also increase your abilities to solve conflicts confidently.

Ridding Your Mind of Irrational Bias

Bias is something that clouds judgment. It may cloud judgment positively or negatively, affecting the way that you evaluate others and the efforts that you put forth in your relationship with them. By using the following strategies, you can become aware of possible bias in the way you view others.

Jumping into conclusions is very easy, especially since our subconscious mind is trained to look for patterns that it recognizes from other life experiences and relay that information back to your brain. For example, someone who has been cheated on in a previous relationship may have a hard time trusting. When their current partner distances themselves for the week before their birthday, they may assume the worst. Likewise, someone who is friends with their boss may become worried when their boss does not greet them as they customarily do in the mornings. In these two scenarios, this can cause them to assume their partner is cheating or that they did something that disappointed or angered their boss. However, the reality may be that their partner is busy working extra hours or planning a surprise for their upcoming birthday or that their boss just received bad news and is not feeling social that day.

When you assume things, you give yourself a limited window to see things. This can apply to certain scenarios like those addressed above, as well as general assumptions that you make about someone's personality. For example, a woman in the business field might come across as cold, which discourages employees from approaching her to ask for help. However, she may be trying to come across as strong. The coldness that she puts off may not be her personality at all — but a way of appearing strong in a male-dominated world of business. By assuming this woman is cold, employees may not ask questions, so they may not benefit from the knowledge she has to offer. It can also cause problems with communication in the business world.

Even though emotional intelligence makes it more likely that you will make accurate assumptions about people based on their language, body language, and non-verbal communication, it is still possible to find yourself biased because of the subconscious mind. Instead of jumping to conclusions within the first few minutes of meeting somebody, take the time to look for additional clues that help indicate someone's personality.

Push Those around You to Do Better

True leaders understand that their success is a reflection of the people that work for them. When all the employees in an organization are collaborating together, it uplifts the entire organization. The best companies to work for are those that take an interest in their employees. Countless studies have proven that employee happiness and productivity contribute to company success. As a leader in the workplace, you should help motivate the people around you to do better.

As an emotionally intelligent person, you should feel confident in your position in the workplace. The employees that work under you are not trying to take your job — they are simply trying to be the best that they can. The first step to encouraging employees to be better is identifying their strengths and weaknesses. Pay close attention to the way that they work with people around them and what their body language says about their relationship. Notice when they communicate well and areas where employees could improve. Then, encourage the employees to do tasks that challenge their weaknesses. For example, have two people who do not collaborate well work with a member of management on a project to practice those skills. As they learn to collaborate, their usefulness to the work environment also increases.

Evaluate Your Ability to Solve Problems

To evaluate your problem-solving capabilities, think back to the last time you disagreed with someone. What was the end result? Were you satisfied at the end of the conflict? Did you have your own needs met?

Did you take the time to understand the other person's needs and find a solution that left everyone satisfied?

By analyzing the way that you solve conflicts, both at home and in the workplace, you can get a clearer picture of your strengths and faults when it comes to problem-solving. Some common problems that people face are not being able to come up with a creative solution that makes everyone happy, having difficulty communicating their own needs or having trouble understanding the needs of the person they are having a conflict with.

Chapter 11:
Learn to Forgive

How to Forgive Yourself and Forgive Others

We've all made mistakes. There is nobody who can go through life claiming they have never made a mistake since the day they were born. You should embrace the art of forgiving yourself first before you can begin forgiving others. Accept your imperfections because you know those can always be improved.

Holding onto your past and repeatedly beating yourself up over it isn't going to change a thing because it has already happened. You're only human, and if you can accept other people for their flaws, you can certainly start accepting yourself too. Forgiving yourself is the simple part of the process; forgiving others is harder to wrap your head around. When someone has hurt us, especially if the hurt runs deep, it can be hard just to let go and let things go back to the way they were. Sometimes even the thought of the incident that happened is enough to bring all those feelings of hurt flooding right back into your mind, even if it is something that happened years ago.

Steps of forgiving those who hurt you in the past may include:

- **By Moving On** – We know this is easier said than done, but it is the only way to begin learning to forgive. Realize that holding onto the past is only hurting you, not them. You are the one that is affected by it. Your emotions are the ones being tormented over the thought of it. However, much you place your thoughts on it, it is never going to change what happened. No amount of dwelling on the past ever will. The best thing for you is just to learn to let go, leave the past behind where it belongs and focus on looking ahead, the way emotionally intelligent people do.

- **Never Go to Bed Angry** – This is one exercise you should start adopting every night from now on. Make it a habit to never go to bed again with negative emotion. It is simply not worth it. If there is nothing you can do to change it, then let it be. Why torture your emotions anymore over something that is never going to change? It's an unhealthy habit. Do, watch or read something that lifts your spirits and puts you in a happy mood before going to bed every night. Remind yourself of all the things you have to be grateful for.

- **Accepting Responsibility** – When confrontations and conflicts occur, it takes two people to rock the boat. While the other person may have had a bigger part to play in the falling out, you were also partially responsible on some level. Being someone with high EQ means that you need to use self-awareness to assess the situation objectively, to be able to see what mistakes you made and how you could have handled that better. From there, accept responsibility for the part that you played, and realize that both people involved were at fault to a certain degree.

- **Choose to Be Kind Instead** – Do you have the desire to be right all the time? Even if it means jeopardizing a relationship because you stubbornly refuse to let go of the need to be right? Such could be the reason why you're finding it hard to forgive. Instead of choosing to be right all the time, choose the emotionally intelligent way. Choose to be kind. Being a kind person is much better than being someone who is 'right'" all the time.

Forgive in Order to Move Forward

There is a saying that says, "Screw me once and it is on me but screw me twice then it is on you." There exists another saying that states "choose your battles wisely." Both are sayings emotionally intelligent people have learned and have become aware of.

Forgiveness involves letting go of everything that happened, regardless of whether it is strike one or strike two.

Forgiving is necessary in order to move on; however, it in no way means that you are giving the other person another chance or the opportunity to chalk up another strike against you. Emotionally intelligent people recognize when it is necessary to 'get along' and move past another's mistake. However, EQ's also recognize when it is also necessary to keep the wrongdoers at 'arm's length' to control the potential harm that the wrongdoer is ever capable of repeating.

Emotionally intelligent people have learned that by not forgiving a perpetual wrongdoer, breeds unchecked and unnecessary emotions that can create unnecessary battles. Digging your heels in to fight a losing battle is counter-productive and can result in irreparable and avoidable harm. Knowing your emotions allows you to choose your battles wisely and enables you to stand your ground just as wisely.

Emotionally intelligent people also realize the counter-productive-ness with hanging out with negative people; including those that choose to complain about things rather than advancing past those things.

Emotionally intelligent people care about people including those that complain, EQ's also know when to 'draw the line' by asking the complainer what their plans are for implementing chosen solutions.

Emotionally intelligent people will be the first to forgive others because they know that circumstances differ for everyone and there may have been reasons why someone did what they did. The world at large is much bigger than what goes on in your head and emotionally intelligent people know this. The reason I suggested meditation as the first step toward emotional intelligence is that it helps you to see things in perspective, slows down your anger and negative feelings and helps you to be able to assess each individual situation using something people don't seem to use much anymore – intuition. When you unlock your intuition, you can trust it because it is there to safe-guard you and it helps you to be able to see beyond the obvious.

People who have a high level of emotional intelligence will be calm people who are not quick to judge others, who can forgive easily and who understand that their own actions actually dictate the outcome of a situation. They tend not to blame others but instead look into themselves to see what could be done to improve any given situation. That's the difference between them and ordinary people whose level of emotional intelligence is low.

Chapter 12:
Emotional Intelligence in Leaders

I'm going to discuss the role of Emotional Intelligence on leadership and professional work later in the chapter in more depth, but it's worth mentioning it here in brief now.

As Daniel Goleman said, *"People do not leave the company, people leave bad bosses."*

Strong Emotional Intelligence enables people to understand what motivates our staff and positively, helping to improve the bond. It's a misnomer that people are motivated by only money or recognition; motivation is much more complicated than that, driven from both the external and the internal. If, as a boss you can recognize a person's individual motivations, you can appeal to them in the most effective way.

An effective leader with strong EQ skills can also identify the needs of his people and address them in a way that boosts performance and workplace satisfaction. Recognizing people's emotions can also help a talented leader build a strong team taking advantage of the emotional range of the people around him.

Our Children

It's fair to say that we learn a great deal of our Emotional Intelligence in childhood because of interaction with our parents. It can start early in our formative years where consoling a crying child, for instance, teaches them they can trust you and the world around them and helps to ease their anxiety.

The tone your family sets around emotions can influence a child and follow them into adulthood. If emotions are something to be denied or shameful, it becomes extremely difficult for a child to learn how to identify and manage their own emotions, or how to respond to others'. They are much more likely to try to hide or dampen down their emotions, meaning they can grow up ending into adults who possess poor Emotional Intelligence.

According to child clinical psychologist, Dr. Tali Shenfield, the best way to help your child to learn strong Emotional Intelligence skills is to accept and acknowledge their emotions, both positive and negative, and to empathize with them. Talking about their feelings, as opposed to trying to distract or deny them, teaches them that emotions are okay. Giving them time to process and manage their emotions and giving them the means to do so (such as giving them the words they need to express themselves) will help them to develop a strong Emotional Intelligence.

A strong EQ will help your son or daughter in childhood as well as later in adulthood.

Relationship guru *Dr. Jeffrey Bernstein* says EQ is a key predictor of a child's ability to forge peer relationships, to bond with his or her family, to reach academic potential at school and to develop a well-balanced outlook.

A child who scores high on EQ usually has an even nature and an accurate outlook of themselves. As they grow older, they can work through age-related challenges and recover from setbacks, either alone or with help. In short, they will become much happier and healthier individuals; what more could we want for our children?

Of course, it's hard to do all the above without strong Emotional Intelligence skills of your own and you may be worrying whether yours are good enough. We all worry at times about failing our children but as I have said before and will keep repeating, the good news is that Emotional Intelligence can be learned.

Why are some individuals more successful than the rest? What is it that makes them leaders who stand out in the crowd? Their work ethic and personality could be contributing factors, but that is only part of the story. The other is the *emotional intelligence* that they possess. In simpler terms, think of EQ as being *street smart*. This is the quality that enables you to navigate through life effectively, and this is the exact quality that you need to develop if you want to find yourself in a leadership position one day.

A successful leader and manager is one that can bring out the best in everyone that they work with. When you have emotional intelligence, it shows. You're more confident, determined, passionate, hardworking, and flexible to the point that you can readily adapt when the situation calls for it. You think on your feet, recover quickly from stress, and remain calm even in the most challenging situations. Being a leader is not an enviable position. There's a huge responsibility that comes with it, and when something goes wrong, you are the one that people turn to for answers and solutions.

The Characteristics of Someone with High EQ

No firm succeeds without the right kind of leadership at the helm. Being a leader and being an effective and successful leader are two different things; one is going to be the head of a company that will just be mediocre, but the other will head a company that is destined for success.

A leader with high emotional intelligence displays the following qualities:

- **They Love Meeting New People** – They have cultivated their curiosity to the point that they never shy away from meeting new people. In fact, they have come to love it. They ask many questions, make a person feel at ease and welcomed, exhibit empathy, and are attuned to the feelings of the other person – even if they may be strangers. This is what someone with high EQ looks like.

- **They Are Attentive** – High EQ individuals are not easily distracted. They are focused, and they can see the bigger picture. They rarely settle for instant gratification. They are attentive and present to their current situation, themselves, and the people that surround them. This is self-awareness in play. They can focus and concentrate on what they are supposed to do, and they do not stop until the goal has been accomplished – no matter the obstacle.

- **They Know Their Strengths** – High EQ enables the ability to be honest with yourself. Exceptional leaders know their strengths and weaknesses, and they embrace both of these with open arms. They don't make excuses for their weakness; they find ways to work on improving them. Not only can they identify their own strengths and weaknesses, but they can also do the same for others that they work with. In a team setting, they know how to identify each team member's area of strength and use that to benefit the team.

- **They Know Why They're Upset** – Leaders always know exactly what the emotional problem is. Not just in themselves, but in others too. This is because they have fine-tuned their self-awareness ability to recognize their emotions so well that they can always recognize *why* they may be upset. They have developed the ability to recognize these emotions as they come up and identify them accurately. Moreover, because they are emotionally intelligent, they can take a step back and make an objective reflection about how the emotion is affecting them.

- **When They Fall, They Rise Again** – A leader never gives up. It is the way that they deal with mistakes which says a lot about what high EQ can do for a person. They know that giving up is never an option, and they know what it takes to get back on the horse and keep marching forward. They are resilient, determined, and never entertain negative emotions because they know it is only a distraction. They never let their motivation dwindle, thanks to high EQ.

- **They Create a Safe Space** – Leaders understand that everyone needs to feel comfortable enough to voice their opinions and concerns. If they are having difficulty working with someone else, they need to feel comfortable enough to approach you – the leader – and bring up those concerns without worrying that there are going to be repercussions for themselves. As a leader, you need to establish yourself as a trustworthy figure and encourage an open-door policy among the people you are managing – encouraging them and making them feel safe whenever they approach you with a problem of their own (knowing that you won't use such information against them at any given moment).

How to Use Emotional Intelligence to Lead Effectively

A leader of a successful company is one that can effectively manage their team and bring out the best in everyone that is under their guidance. A successful leader and manager are one that can bring out the best in everyone that they work with. A good leader is one that knows how to spearhead the journey to success.

Use emotional intelligence to become an effective leader by:

- **Displaying Mutual Respect** – Respect is one of the major principles that absolutely must be present within a team and an organization. Respect among managers and co-workers is the glue that keeps the company successful, and without it, things can unravel really quickly. Use empathy, self-awareness and social skills to help you foster mutual respect. The best type of leaders are ones that provide a work environment where employees help each other and value the contributions that each individual makes. Effective leaders constantly encourage their peers to bring their A-game to work every day and help them overcome the challenges faced in the workplace without belittling them.

- **Welcoming Diversity** – If you want to be an effective leader that solves problems for good, you need to tailor your solutions depending on the person you are dealing with. Self- awareness, empathy and social skills again come into play here. Use this high EQ trait to treat the individuals in your team just as they are – individuals.

- **Effectively Managing Conflict** – If there is one thing that nobody wants to deal with, it is conflict, especially conflict in the workplace because it really brings down morale and leads to miserable staff if not dealt with accordingly. Nobody wants to deal with conflict, but as a leader, you are going to have to. A leader with high EQ is going to depend on empathy, self-regulation, self-awareness, and social skills to help them with this. An effective leader will never turn a blind eye to conflict and will do everything in their power to address the conflict as soon as it rears its ugly head and resolve it in the most amicable way possible.

- **Engaging with People** – When you engage with your team members, as a leader, you need to go the extra mile and make a connection with each member of your team. This helps build a relationship that is meaningful and shows your team members you genuinely care about them and their welfare – not just because it is part of your job to do so. Rely on social skills, empathy, and self-awareness for this category.

- **Recognize Each Person for What They Are** – In a work environment especially, sometimes a leader can be so focused on expecting employees to be more like them that they forget to appreciate what makes that employee unique. There is nothing that de-motivates a team quicker than feeling like they are not appreciated. When they start to feel de-motivated, they begin to lose the passion and the drive to really strive to perform. An effective leader will use their emotional intelligence skills (social and empathy) to recognize each employee's contribution and work with them on developing their individual strengths. They recognize each employee for what they are, and they never expect them to be something that they are not.

- **Making Trust a Priority** – Without trust, there is no possibility of working together well. For a leader to be considered successful, they must cultivate an environment of trust at all times. You are leading others who have placed their faith in you, and you should return that faith by being as transparent, honest and open as possible. Use social skills and empathy as your guiding points, learn how to read the emotions of others well, and you will have no problems making trust a priority.

- **Being Empathic Always** – A successful leader is one who can practice empathy and compassion with sincerity. High EQ skills will enable you to do this. People are more acute at spotting insincerity than you think, no matter how good of an actor you think you are. Part of being a transparent leader means being honest not just verbally, but also with your feelings too.

- **Listening Actively** – A successful leader is one that has learned to listen intently, and not just to what the person has to say, but beyond that. For example, when having a one-on-one conversation, listen to the voice inflections, the tone of the person's voice, which words they emphasize on, and how they sound when they are expressing what they feel. This is where empathy is going to play a huge role because it is a valuable high EQ skill which is going to help you really connect with the person you're speaking to. Be emphatic towards them, compassionate, understanding and nurturing appropriately. Don't just listen to what they are saying, but listen to what they are trying to tell you and tune in to them in a way many leaders fail to do today.

How Emotional Intelligence Can Increase Your Chances of Success

To improve the quality of your life, you need to have emotional intelligence on your side. This is the key trait of making a difference. No shortcuts. No secret weapons. No magic formulas. Just developing high levels of EQ.

To achieve success in general, here is how EQ is going to play a huge role in helping you achieve that. How often have you set goals, raised the bar, and had big dreams only to have life getting in the way? Your emotions get worked up through stress, and all your initial desire to succeed just comes crashing to a halt. When someone lacks EQ, they tend to become more reactive than proactive. They are unable to adapt to the situations as they come. The experiences affect them more than they should, and they become far too overwhelmed by the wave of emotions that crash around them. This is precisely why you need EQ.

EQ trains you to manage your emotions in healthy ways. It enables you to reign in impulsive behaviors, manage your expectations and adapt to the unexpected that happens. This is how you succeed. The ability to understand your emotions is half the EQ battle, and if you can achieve this portion, you've already won (almost). The other half is, of course, learning how to understand and manage the emotions of other people. Obstacles are the biggest reason many fail to reach the goals they have set, because the challenges, the setbacks, disappointments, and failure can often strip you of the will you need to keep going – especially if you don't know how to regulate your emotions.

Here are other ways emotional intelligence can increase your chances of success:

- **It Helps You Predict Performance** – EQ has a significant impact on success because it helps you focus on results which matter. When you focus on the results, your performance is instantly given a boost, and thanks to self-awareness, you will be able to predict your actions and reactions to the situations you may be facing.

- **It Leaves No Room for Negativity** – When you've got high EQ, there is no room for any element that threatens success. Negativity becomes a thing of the past.

- **It Makes You Hungry for Success** – As we have already established, high EQ individuals never lose sight of their motivation, and they use their self-awareness and self-regulation to manage their emotions when they are faced with difficult circumstances. This ensures that the desire to quit is never stronger than the desire for success.

- **It Helps You Be Mindful** – It helps one to become aware of their thoughts and be in control.

- **It Helps You Minimize Stress** –With so much internal burden to carry around, how would you focus on achieving success? This is why high EQ makes a difference – because of how it helps you regulate your emotions and manage them properly. Minimizing your stress means you will now have the mental clarity that is needed to start thinking about the next step you need to take.

- **It Improves Your Self-Esteem** – Something that so many of us struggle with. It is impossible to succeed with low self-esteem because you simply do not believe in yourself enough. Possibly one of the best benefits of improving your EQ is how much it is going to improve your self-esteem in the long run. When you begin to continually pursue betterment in your life, you'll find more things to be happy about, which leads to higher levels of satisfaction – improving the way you feel about yourself and thereby enhancing your self-esteem. The constant pursuit of betterment is an example of you succeeding in life in general.

- **It Makes It Easier to Spot Opportunities** – Being self-aware has so many benefits, and not just because it helps you manage your emotions better. When you are more attuned to your surroundings, yourself and the people around you, it becomes easier to notice the opportunities that you may not otherwise have spotted. Negativity and a lack of EQ often cloud our judgment and perception, which is why successful people strive to develop emotional intelligence skills for themselves, so their eyes will be opened to start noticing solutions rather than problems.

- **It Empowers You** – As you learn to manage your emotions better, you start regaining confidence in yourself once more. As your confidence and self-esteem improve, with each challenge you successfully overcome with self-awareness and self-regulation, empathy, motivation, and social skills, you'll find yourself becoming more empowered, stronger, and capable of absolutely anything you set your heart and mind to. You feel like there is nothing that will hold you back, as you see each goal you set materialize before you when you smash through them, and this will serve as your fuel when your build momentum towards transforming your life.

- **It Makes You a Better Version of Yourself** – When you've adopted all the core principles that make high EQ such a desirable trait, without even realizing you're going to put in the effort to become better than what you are right now. You'll start focusing on having a passion and a purpose, and you take the necessary steps that you need to improve the things that you don't want in your life. This is what it means to be successful, to become the best version of yourself that you can possibly be.

- **It Helps You Stay Committed to the End** – Giving up is no longer an option because you've learned how to regulate your responses whenever that feeling arises. When you set a goal with high EQ, you're not only creating a goal; you're committing to seeing it through. This commitment is exactly what helps you stay productive because you're able to regulate your emotions to control your reactions and your outcome. Success would not be possible without the desire to be committed to the end.

Chapter 13:
Myths Debunked

The False Ideas You Need to Shed About Being an Empath

There are so many myths and false concepts that have circulated over the years around being an empath and I feel many of these ideas actually make it hard for us to live empowered lives. Let's start debunking a few of these and see if any of them hit a nerve for you.

False Idea #1: Is being an empath a totally spiritual thing?

This is definitely a basic misconception that segregates empaths. While the lines do sometimes cross over between science and spirituality, you absolutely don't need to be spiritual, religious or a spiritual healer to be an empath.

My Truth:

Scientific research has proven the existence of empaths. To be fair, this is a very new study in the world of science and we barely understand the neurology behind empathy in general. But new research is surfacing supporting the existence of empaths. Though we still have a long way to go, findings are showing between one and two percent of the population does report experiencing conditions associated with being empathic.

And the fact still holds true. My brain will demonstrate empathic abilities whether I'm spiritually inclined or not. Therefore, understanding empaths isn't supposed to be some esoteric wishy-washy impractical thing.

False Idea #2: Are empathic abilities a disorder or mental illness?

While it is true that we often get hit with overwhelming situations and scenarios that leave us feeling physically sick, it is certainly not true that empaths suffer from mental disorders or anything of that kind.

My Truth:

The emotions and physical sensations you have are nothing to be ashamed of. There is nothing wrong with you! You are not sick or crazy.

Let me say that again...

Don't be put to shame or feel less than because you possess abilities to perceive far greater things than the general public. The human population has become so desensitized it's easier to label and categorize those groups of people that don't fit into the model view of the status quo such as empath who possess powers of higher perception.

False Idea #3: Does being an empath mean you're weak and playing the victim?

Emotions are for wimps and overly sensitive people. I bet you've heard that all your life. This false belief has been pervading human consciousness for centuries. Showing your emotions is often seen as a sign of weakness. A lot of people assume that empaths are weak, powerless and co-dependent on others. Many believe empaths live in a state of victimhood always fearful of the world around them.

Revealing to people your truth and what you can sense in them is so scary for people that are disconnected from their own emotions, they often call you a freak. Perhaps this is why most empaths become recluse.

My Truth:

All these misconceptions are generalized biases and nothing close to the truth. The fact that we can quickly process emotions and sensations that the majority of the population does not understand doesn't mean we are weaker. If anything, we pay more attention to the feelings of others and pay a lot of attention to how we treat others. There's no need for you ever to justify or get offended when someone rejects who you are. Just remember for most people, your way of being is incomprehensible and illogical to their mind.

When it comes to taking responsibility, bouncing back from challenges and working hard to make a difference, empaths perform just as well as any other human being. An empath can be just as strong, responsible and successful in the world as anyone else, so don't let other people's limitations or fears cause you to settle for anything less than what your heart desires.

False Idea #4: Are all empaths introverts?

It appears to be that most empaths happen to be introverts but this is certainly not true across the board.

My Truth:

Individuals bearing all kinds of characteristics will possess empathic abilities. Don't feel like you have to 'fit' into a particular category of anything in order to exercise your empathic gifts. You can be an extrovert, introvert, ambivert or none of the above and still be an empath.

The idea of introversion as a pre-requisite for being termed an empath is simply not true.

Now that you've shed some of the false notions that may have played a role in constricting you, take a moment to see if any other myths come up. I encourage you to write them down on a piece of paper and right next to them write your truth. Convert all the active false beliefs in your mind about what it means to be an empath into constructive ideas that will nourish a healthy mindset.

Conclusion

Emotional intelligence is something that can be cultivated simply by stopping and thinking as you go about your life. Be more aware of your own emotions and the emotions of the people around you. When you are stressed or experience conflict, learn to pinpoint the root cause of the problem and then work to find a solution.

As you hone your emotional intelligence skills, you will find that the quality of your relationships and your role at work starts to change. As you identify the things that you need, as well as the things that the people around you need, you will find a better sense of balance in life.

With conscious effort, your emotional intelligence will rise naturally. Even confirmatory tests, you will notice the difference in the way that you think and feel. You will also notice a difference in your relationships with your coworkers, friends, and family members.

Best of luck on your journey to higher emotional intelligence and self-improvement!

If you find this book helpful in anyway a review to support my endeavors is much appreciated.

Robin T. Schneider